# Land of the Lost

## Exploring the Vanished Townships
## of the North-east of Scotland

To Evis and Alistair
who walked in the
Land of the Lost

# Land of the Lost

## Exploring the Vanished Townships of the North-east of Scotland

ROBERT SMITH

JOHN DONALD PUBLISHERS LTD
EDINBURGH

ISBN 0 85976 477 X

*British Library Cataloguing in Publication Data.*

A catalogue record for this book is available
from the British Library.

Typesetting and prepress origination by Brinnoven, Livingston.
Printed & bound in Great Britain by Bell & Bain Ltd, Glasgow.

# CONTENTS

# INTRODUCTION

The little hamlet of Bellabeg lies seven miles east of Corgarff, a scattered community on the road that runs through Strathdon from Kildrummy to the Lecht. The parish was originally called Invernochty, for this is where the Water of Nochty comes tumbling down from the Ladder hills and empties itself into the Don. Bellabeg has a school, a general store, a garage, a post office and little else, but two things have put it on the map. One is the famous Lonach Gathering, where whisky is known to flow as freely as the Nochty Water. The other is a road sign — 'Lost'.

'Lost' is a farm in Glen Nochty, not far from the main road. Beyond it, a rutted farm track pushes north to the distant hills, following the Nochty Water past the deserted farm of Belnabodach, the 'town of the ghost', and on by Corriebreck to the ruined mansion of Auchernach. Here, the name 'Lost' takes on a different meaning. The *larach* [ruins] and broken dykes tell you what has really been lost in these remote glens.

This was driven home to me a few years ago when I stood at Lost with old Charlie Gordon, whose family had run the farm for 200 years. The origin of the name is uncertain, but the place-name experts say it comes from the Gaelic *Feith na Loiside,* meaning 'marsh of the loisid or kneading trough'. Charlie thought the original name was Losset, which meant 'a small meeting place'; it seemed more convincing than any theory about kneading troughs.

Charlie was eighty-five when I met him, a fine old man, but now he has gone and his farm is run by his son George. I can still see him standing there, talking about the old days, leaning on his stick, lifting it and pointing it up the glen, 'I can remember,' he said, 'when there were forty reekin' lums up there.' Forty reekin' lums…it was a phrase I was to hear time and again. It said more about the depopulation of the glens than any long-winded report.

Charlie's reekin' lums were symbols of a way of life that reached back through the centuries. Today, the only reminders of that forgotten age are the ruins of crumbling settlements and old shiels hidden away in the hills of Donside and Deeside, scattered across the Cabrach moors and up the River A'an, spaced out like markers along old drove roads and tucked away on the banks of countless burns.

Hunger and poverty drove the people from these 'lost' communities. In the 'ill years' of the late 18th century when famine lay over the land like a plague, it was said that half the people in some Deeside parishes died from hunger. In the 1740s bitter frosts ravaged the crops so badly that every ninth person in Crathie and Braemar was destitute, while up in Strathspey families were eating nettles, mugwort and turnip-thinnings.

There were conflicting views on the part played by the lairds in the depopulation of the glens. Evictions on Deeside rarely matched the scale of the Highland Clearances, but the Deeside chronicler, John Grant Michie, minister of Dinnet, said it was less severe because it was a gradual dispossession over a much longer period. Nevertheless, it happened. 'The spectacle of a band of evicted families from the upper glens of Braemar passing through the long strath, with sorrow and sadness depicted in every face, and headed by a piper playing "Lochaber no more", was not likely soon to be forgotten.'

Evictions, famine, army recruiting...they all added up to a steady erosion of life in the glens. In *The Cairngorms,* Nethersole-Thomson and Adam Watson gave population figures for Strathdon and for Glen Muick, Tullich and Glen Gairn. Together, they totalled 4,020 in 1755, dropping to 3,357 by 1811. In Crathie and Braemar the population fell from 2,671 to 2,251 between 1755 and 1791.

'The remote parts were first to lose their people,' they said. 'Glen Fernait [in Atholl], with twenty-two clachan clusters in the late 18th century was virtually deserted by the late 19th century. Last century there were few or no compulsive evictions or clearances in any of these districts, except Glen Ey, but the end result was the same: empty houses but no voices on the braes. The ruins of scores of clachans are still there in Glen Gairn, Glen Clunie, Aberarder, Bridge of Brown, Dorback, Glen Esk and Glen Fernait.'

It is difficult to imagine them when there were voices on the braes. What were they like, these 'clachan clusters'? John Grant Michie said that in the early 19th century cottar houses could hardly be distinguished from the surrounding heath-covered hillocks. They were simply 'rough stones piled on top of one another, the cavities filled with sods', and they were set in 'uncouth wastes of bog and heath'.

# INTRODUCTION

The clachans were usually built near water. In *Northern Life,* William Alexander, whose father was a crofter and blacksmith in the Chapel of Garioch, said more romantically, that they were sited by 'a gushing spring of caller water' or by some 'wimplin' burnie'. Despite his cosy references to 'gladsome daylight' and 'goodly trees', Alexander gave an accurate and carefully detailed description of the old houses, built of 'feal' or turf, heather or dub, or mud and straw. He described the watlin which carried the divots and the 'thack' fastened on with 'strae rapes'.

The number of houses varied from four or five to a dozen, some with a barn or byre 'planted down as if they had been dropt from the clouds'. In some districts the style of building was known as 'Auchenhalrig' after a place in Moray where it was first tried out. The description of the Auchenhalrig technique reads like a do-it-yourself manual for 19th-century clachan builders.

It took thirty cartloads of stones, ten cartloads of clay or mud, and twenty-four stones weight of good fresh straw. When the straw and mud were properly worked together they gave a thickness of 22 inches, sufficient for a wall 7 feet in height. The walls, 'when properly built and kept well under thatch', would last for more than a century.

*Land of the Lost* tells the story of these old crofting communities — tiny hamlets and clachans that are now no more than names on a map — some not even that. It tells, too, about the shielings to which the crofters and families migrated with their cattle for the summer grazing. The book is about a unique breed of people who lived out their lives there, struggling against sickness and starvation, cultivating 'poverty-stricken ridges of land', coping with crude, uncomfortable sod-walled houses and roads that were 'inconceivably bad', fighting intractable lairds. In the end, they lost.

It is also about the people who live there today, people like Peter Goodfellow, an artist who has his own 'Lost' land in Glen Nochty, and Wullie Gray, the Bard of Corgarff, and *his* lost clachan, about old Willie Thomson, who told me about the mysterious Delfrankie, and Rab Bain, who lives on a hilltop and once told me, 'I've got twa teeth an' my dog has a'e e'e'.'

But above all it is a book that searches for a sense of the past, looking at old days and old ways, and hoping, perhaps, to catch a whisper of those 'voices on the braes'.

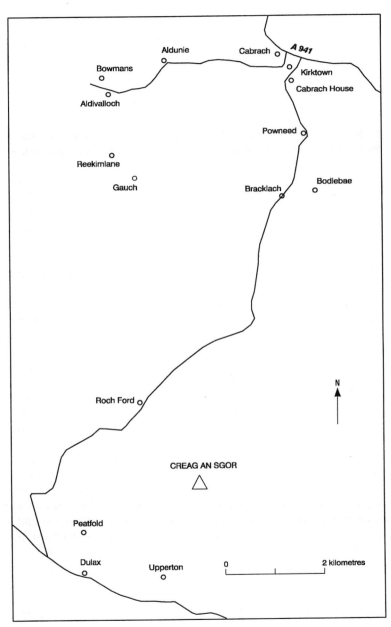

*Map 1. This map covers old settlements lying between the Cabrach and Glenbuchat. The route by the Roch Ford once linked the two communities.*

# CHAPTER I
# BACKSIDE OF THE WORLD

**U**p on Creag an Sgor, the Craig of the Sharp Rock, I had the wind on my face and the cold, bleak world at my feet, I had come up from Dulax, a deserted farm in Glen Buchat, on a day when frost whitened the paling posts and the first snow of winter lay across the hills. I was following an old peat road over the shoulder of the hill and down to the Roch Ford, a crossing of the Howe Water at the head of the Deveron. Behind me lay Peatfold, where the ruins of a clachan could still be seen in the heather. To the north was the Blackwater Forest and the Cabrach.

The Roch Ford was once a gateway to the Cabrach. In the days before Highland Games came into vogue this was where men from Glen Buchat and the Cabrach came together to match their strength at the Lifting Stones. The stones, which lay on the south side of the ford, varied in size and weight and had to be raised and piled on top of a pointed rock. I found a number of large stones on a track running down to the ford, but whether or not they were the original Lifting Stones was anybody's guess.

When you cross the Roch Ford and head into the Cabrach you are entering a harsh, uncompromising land where the very names intimidate you...Scad Hill, a bare scabbed hill that nudges the Buck; Clayhooter Hill, from the word hooter or hotter, 'a quaking, moving mass'; Thiefsbush Hill and Thunderclap Hill; Powneed, the pool of the nest, a swampy place near Bracklach; and Gauch a windy place.

A 19th-century traveller, J G Philips, author of *Wanderings in the Highlands,* came into the Cabrach from Glenlivet by the Steplar trail and wrote about 'rents of rain' and a mist that shut out hill and glen, rock and stream, earth and sky. 'All around was dim semi-darkness,' he said. This was known as 'black weet'. There was also 'white weet' — snow. It was once said that it 'dang doon black weet' for six weeks in the Cabrach. Philips saw it as 'a barren desert, where no creature lived'. Yet people did live there. He caught a glimpse of a house a long way off in a gap between two hills. This was Cairnbrallan, the home of a gamekeeper on the edge of the Black Water, deep in the Cabrach wilderness. Today it is a ruin.

1

*Ruined cottar house at Cabrach. Buck of Cabrach in background.*

The Cabrach is pock-marked with the remains of abandoned farms and cottar houses. They can be seen as you drive up the road from Rhynie to Dufftown and along the more remote Auchindoir road. Early in 1996, the Royal Commission on the Ancient and Historical Monuments of Scotland carried out a survey at the ruined farmstead of Bogs on the Craig estate, which lies off the Auchindoir road. Bogs was in use in 1870 but was abandoned at the end of the century. They found that the farm was on the edge of an earlier and more extensive settlement, comprising a dozen or more buildings.

When I was in the Cabrach I met Charlie Gordon, who lives with his brother Hugh at Dykeside, near the kirkton. He has seen depopulation taking its toll on the countryside. He says it is still going on; that closures are still taking place, that farms are still being allowed to collapse into heaps of rubble and that houses which become unoccupied tend to stay that way. The clearing of the Cabrach isn't always left to Nature.

From the back door of his cottage at Dykeside, Charlie can see across the fields to where a farm hugs the lower slopes of the Hill of Bank. J G Philips stayed at the farm, the Bank of Corinacy, when

*Jimmie Shiach (right) and Charles Gordon at the gate at Auchmair.*

in the Cabrach. In those days the farmer had a herd of over 200 cattle and a stock of blackfaced sheep totalling from 500 to 700. In his *Wanderings* he described how fields rich with a mass of waving yellow grain were ravaged by an overnight storm. 'The fiend of destruction had passed over the Cabrach,' he wrote. In time, that 'fiend' created more destruction than he could have imagined, for today, like so many other farms, the Bank is a ruin, abandoned and forgotten.

The Bank's neighbour is Auchmair, a sturdy old-fashioned farm-house built to withstand the Cabrach winds. Bluff, burly Jimmy Shiach has farmed there for the past thirty years, He has had his ups-and-downs; he says there was a time when he was in the Slough of Despond, but he appreciates what he has got and sends up a prayer of thanks for it. It takes the shape of large metal letters on his roadside gate which say — 'Auchmair — May the Lord be praised'. He was once a shepherd, watching over flocks on the summer grazing at Corgarff and wintering at his home in Keith, Now he follows the same pattern on his farm, flitting between the Cabrach and Keith with the changing seasons.

We stood on the brae at Auchmair looking out across the flat peaty countryside to where the Buck stood guard on the Cabrach. We were talking about the old days and how things had changed.

*Charlie Gordon ploughing with a horse and a stot.*

'Show him the oxen plough,' Jimmy told Charlie Gordon, who went off to Dykeside to dig out a photograph which pictured him at the plough. Instead of the usual pair of horse, there was only one horse — and a stot. The stot [young bull] was called Jack and the horse was called Star. Charlie pointed at the figure behind the plough. 'That's me fin I wis sixteen,' he said. 'It wis my first fee.'

The year was 1944. Charlie couldn't remember why they had to use a stot. Maybe it had something to do with the war, or maybe, Jimmy thought, it was because a lot of farm horses had been stricken with grass sickness that year. Yet at one time the use of oxen was commonplace. In the days of the run-rigs, when the land was 'ridged like the waves of the sea', teams of cattle and horses were used to pull the massive Scots plough. Joint tenants in a farmtoun each supplied an ox for the plough.

I left Auchmair and its memories and went off to the Kirktown, past the market stance where as recently as ten years ago big annual sheep sales were held. Charlie's old school was opposite the post office. It had thirty pupils when he was there before the war; now it is closed down, looking tawdry and neglected. I was told that the school in the Lower Cabrach had only seven pupils. When I was at the Kirkton there was word that the Upper Cabrach Post office was also closing.

From the Kirktown a road goes west to Aldunie, crossing the Allt Deveron near the Upper Cabrach church. The present church dates from 1786. I wandered about the old graveyard, searching among the tombstones for names and places that might bring the past into closer focus. I half-expected to see the grave of the Rev John Irving, who was ordained in 1666 and was so popular with his parishioners that he was called 'a dwarf and rogge' and a 'dwarf bodie', but he was deposed in 1677.

I saw a tablestone marking the grave of Alexander Scott, of Aldunie, who died in the 1830s. It carried a chilling message for the living:

> Reader be admonished!
> You are moving on to meet
> the King of Terrors.

I was told of an old man on his death-bed who was asked by the minister if he was ready to meet the King of Terrors. He replied sourly: 'I might well be, for I've lived now for forty years with the Queen of Terrors.'

Scotts, Shaws, Souters, Bains, Roys, Gordons and Sheeds were among the names I saw. One comparatively recent stone carried the name of John Sheed of Aldunie, who died in January, 1990, aged seventy-seven. It came as a shock to me. Nearly a decade before, I had met John on my first visit to Aldunie. Now he was gone and another generation of Sheeds had taken over.

I wondered what changes had taken place since then, and I wondered, too, what sort of people they had been, these crofters and cottars who had lived out their lives in the lonely reaches of the Deveron and the Black Water. In 1875, Alexander Smith, in his *New History of Aberdeenshire,* said they were well known to be shrewd dealers in black cattle and sheep.' None have been hanged or banished in modern times,' he wrote. But hanging and banishment weren't the only things that drove people from the Cabrach. Famine, crop failures, bitter frosts and 'great storms of snow and drift' made life almost impossible. The Cabrach was once said to be so desolate and inhospitable that only dire necessity would make people cross it. Priests at a Roman Catholic chapel at Shenval in the Lower Cabrach described it as the 'Siberia of Scotland'.

Farms became derelict, crofts fell into disrepair, and up on the Black Water, in the Cabrach's Siberia, a whole community was wiped from the map. The old village of Horseward disappeared more than a century ago, and now there is nothing left to show that it ever existed. Gradually, ground that had been cultivated by the villagers was covered over by bent and heather, almost as if Nature had shamefacedly drawn a curtain over the scene. Horseward got its name from the ancient custom of turning horses on to common hill pasture during the summer.

The years have seen unremitting decline. In 1831 the population of the parish was 978; by 1901 it had dropped to 581. At the turn of the century it was reported that nearly 100 dwelling-houses in the valley of the Deveron were in ruins, while to the south, in the neighbourhood of Bridgend and Aldivalloch, the creeping rot of depopulation was spreading.

I wanted to find out how Aldivalloch's neighbour, Aldunie, had survived time and the Cabrach weather. Generations of Scotts had farmed there, their links with the community going back to the middle of the 17th century, when the holding was known as Old-downie. For the past half century, however, it had been farmed by the Sheeds. I remember John Sheed telling me that when he came to Aldunie in 1947 all the cottages in the area were occupied. In the thirty years after that twenty families moved out. Now he had gone and his place was been taken by his son David, whose wife, Maureen, is from Tarland. They have two sons, Martin, and Neil, who is in Aberdeen. John's widow, Lizzie, completed the family.

Lizzie Sheed confirmed what her husband had said about the drift from the Cabrach. 'After we came up here', she said, 'a house closed practically every year'. Three homes were occupied in 1947 plus a keeper's house. As far as she knew the Sheed connection with Aldunie went back to 1767, when a James Sheed married a Christian McJames. The Poll Book of 1696 shows that John Gordon married Jannet, daughter of James Sheed, farmer, Aldunie, and died in Reekimlane in 1882. Lizzie Sheed's uncle David was born in a thatched house near Aldunie in 1868, when their present house was being built.

*Martin Sheed, David Sheed, Lizzie Sheed and Maureen Sheed at Aldunie in the Cabrach.*

Aldunie, like all the farms scattered about the Cabrach, has its roots in the old clachans and farmtouns of two or three centuries ago. Gauch, to the south of Aldunie, is given in the Poll Book as 'the said *town* of Geach'. These 'clachan clusters' contained the homes of anything from six to a dozen peasant families, sometimes extended by the hovels of a handful of cottars.

The tenancy or joint tenancy of a farm was held directly from the landowner or tacksman. Below the tenants were subtenants, employed as hinds [ploughman], herds and threshers.

The crofter was marginally better-off than the cottar and grassmen were usually cottars with herding duties. In Aberdeenshire, women were often employed as grasswomen. Today, David Sheed is hind, herd and thresher combined, but, as I learned when I heard the story of his father's boots, he comes from hardy stock. There was a souter in Aldunie when John Sheed worked with *his* father, Alexander Sheed, on the croft of Tomnaven in the Lower Cabrach. The croft was in a remote hill area near the banks of the Deveron — a long way from his home at Aldunie. But John Sheed liked to have his boots shod by the Aldunie souter. When they were in need of repair he would set off from Tomnaven, tramp seven miles to Aldunie, hand in his boots to the souter, and stay with his grannie at Meadow Cottage between Aldunie and Aldivalloch. Next morning, he would pick up the boots and walk all the way back to Tomnaven.

I sat and listened to the Sheeds telling me about the farms that had closed down...Powneed, the Butts, the two Bodiebaes, two farms at Bracklach...on and on it went, a long catalogue of despair. It was as if the 'seven ill years' had returned — the years when famine had torn the heart out of the Cabrach. Now, two-and-a-half centuries later, farms were again being abandoned.

One of the 'lost' fermtouns was Aldivalloch, half a mile south of Aldunie. David Sheed, who works the land at Aldivalloch, said he thought there were seven houses there that had been occupied and three or four in ruins. It was a typical old-style clachan, a cluster of houses on the banks of the Burn of Aldivalloch — *Allt-a-bhealaic,* 'the burn of the pass' — where an ancient right-of-way crosses the hills to Glenlivet. I counted ten buildings, some still roofed, others in ruins. The old 'thackit' houses that had survived now had rusting corrugated iron roofs. The low doors were enclosed in decrepit wooden porches, but there still existed a curious, saddening sense of what life had been like in the old farmtoun. I looked into a but and ben, its windows boarded up, tattered strips of flowered wall-paper on its walls. Outside, real flowers brought a touch of colour to the drab scene. Canterbury bells breaking through a rash of knee-high nettles in what appeared to be a garden.

I walked down to the ford, where a broken wooden footbridge had fallen into the Burn of Aldivalloch. It had once taken travellers across the water to Hillhead of Largue, another ruin, and up the Steplar trail, pushing west to Glenlivet by the Dead Wife's Hillock. When I was there a decade ago John Sheed told me about three peaty mounds which were said to be the hillocks.

It was thought that some woman had died at that spot. Up on the brae behind Aldivalloch was Bowmans, a deserted cottar house. In Aberdeenshire small farmers and cottars were called bowmen, a word derived from the Suio-Gothic *bol,* a village.

From Aldivalloch I went on to Reekimlane. The Cabrach was once the land of black cattle, but now sheep were everywhere, on the track, scattered across the fields, peering out of roofless farm

*Gauch (pronounced 'Jach').*

buildings. I went through gates and deer fences, pushing on to where Creag an Sgor raised its rocky head above the distant hills. In the 'seven ill years' people here had bled their cattle and sheep and mixed it with meal to survive, but in the end they were forced to leave their homes. Only one house remained occupied — and only one lum was reekin. The family there lived by fishing for trout in the local burns.

In a sense, history was repeating itself at Reekimlane, for while farms all over the Cabrach were falling into ruin the old thatched cottage that was Reekimlane had transformed itself into a modern building with white-painted walls, a well set out lawn, and space for parking cars. It is used now only in the summer as a holiday home and when I was there the steading at the rear of the house was being converted to living quarters.

In stark contrast to Reekimlane is Gauch or Geach, the last farm on the road from Aldunie to the Roch Ford. Lizzie Sheed told me that the local pronunciation was Jach. It stands on high ground above the Gauch Burn, looking across to the Balvalley Moss. The farmhouse has been gutted, turned into a barn, with its gable-end opened up to make a huge door. Half the porch was torn away as if it had been ravaged by Cabrach winds.

Behind the house the outlines of other buildings showed that it had been a farmtoun of some size. There were fifteen entries under

'Geach' in the 1696 Poll, including a number of cottars and herds, one a tradesman, and a handful of servants.

There is another track, trodden by generations of Cabrach and Glen Buchat folk, which also links the two communities. It starts at the Kirktown and goes south by Cabrach Lodge, Powneed and Bracklach. When I was there a 'Private' sign had been put up at the Kirkton gate. There was no stile or opening to allow pedestrian access, although in 1997 there was talk that this was to be changed. The barriers had been raised by Christopher Moran, of Golden Lane Securities, Ltd, a London company which owns 41,600 acres of the Cabrach and Glen Fiddich. From what I was told, visitors are discouraged. These are ancient, traditional routes through the Cabrach. They should be open to local people and hillwalkers — to walk them as they please. I did just that.

The Bracklach route, closer to the sweeping contours of the Buck, is the least daunting of the Cabrach passes. Fields stretch away to Upper and Nether Howbog, just off the Dufftown-Rhynie road, while across the peatlands to the west the woods of Aldivaloch and the white walls of Reekimlane can be seen. The first farm is Powneed, where the track drops down to a ford over the Allt Deveron.

J G Philip paid a visit to Powneed, where a Miss Bain served him with tea and 'the finest cheese we have ever seen'. He thought visitors to the Upper Cabrach should call at Powneed. They would find that some things had changed. The farmhouse, which is unoccupied, is in reasonable condition, but the surrounding buildings, including a broken-down railway carriage, tell the same old story. Bracklach, a mile on, is even more melancholy, for it seems to have been a farmtoun of some size and importance. It looks over the squiggling curves of the Allt Deveron to Little Bodiebae and Bodiebae, both ruins.

When I was coming back from the Roch Ford I saw a Land Rover splashing across the ford to Little Bodiebae. The driver was Gary Ferguson, assistant keeper on the Cabrach Estate, a job he had held for only three weeks. There were two guns on the seat beside him. Watching the rabbits scuttling about the moor, he said he would probably shoot one on the way home. He would boil it, throw in a can of Uncle Ben and have it for dinner. He had never seen a rabbit suffering from myxamatosis, so that wouldn't put him off, although, he added thoughtfully, his grannie would never eat it. The Glorious Twelfth was only a week off — he would be thinking of grouse then, not rabbits. He wheeled his Land Rover off the track and bumped up the brae to the farm.

I watched him disappear down the road that led to the Roch Ford. 'He's off to the backside of the world,' I thought. That, at anyrate, was what was said by one traveller, a Dr Michie, when he crossed the Cabrach hills more than a century ago. "I have travelled mony a weary foot through this warl'," he declared, 'but noo I have reached the backside of it.' It may have been an accurate description of the area, but I have come to the conclusion that the Cabrach is much maligned.

This remote corner of the North-east, with its *larachs,* its winds and storms, its loneliness, is often regarded by the outside world as the Land of the Lost. But there is another Cabrach to be seen if you look for it, a place where the skies are vast and blue-hazed hills bring a sense of total tranquility, where 'cuckoo' flowers grow on the edge of the tracks and buttercups throw a golden canopy over the land. 'It's all natural,' said Maureen Sheed. No deadening insecticides here.

I met Maureen again when she was walking down the road from the kirk to Aldunie after laying flowers on the grave of her father-in-law, John Sheed. Her dogs, Fly and Lassie, were with her. Her husband David had told me that she 'took off with the dogs' whenever she was free. When I remarked that the country was looking bonny on that sunny summer's day she replied, 'It's bonny all the year round'. I said I thought the Cabrach had touched *me* with some of its magic. 'It grows on you', she said.

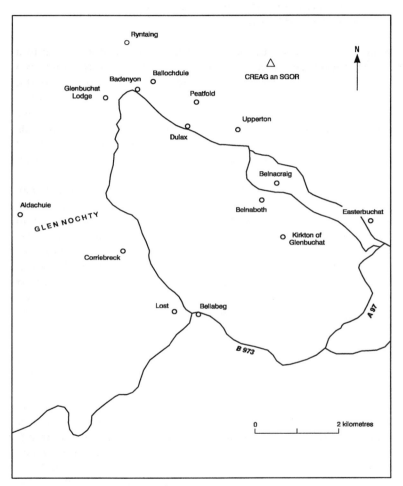

*Map 2. From Easterbuchat the glen runs north to Badenyon, where the road loops south to the farm of Lost and Bellabeg.*

## CHAPTER 2

# CAULD KALE FOR BREAKFAST

**W**hen I set out to explore Glenbuchat I first had to find a forgotten track that would lead me back through two centuries of history. It would take me to shadowy passes where the reivers, those 'wild, scurrilous people', had come riding out of the night, and it would set me on the tracks of the drovers, pushing their cattle to markets in the south. It would carry me past broken walls and ruined mansions, and it would show me where folk had lived in sod-built houses and clawed an impossible living out of an unfriendly land.

I was searching for the Glenbuchat of the past and the gateway to it lay just off the main Strathdon road, less than a mile east of the Bridge of Buchat. Here, a rough farm track climbs up through a field where a crumbling cottar house stands under two sheltering trees. This is all that is left of the Croft of Delfrankie, which is said to have stood on the old route into Glenbuchat, past a small clachan at Easter Buchat and up the dusty road to Badenyon. An inn at Delfrankie served travellers on their way up the glen or heading west to Corgarff and the notorious Lecht Pass.

Delfrankie can be seen on an Ordnance Survey map of Strathdon published in 1869. The Croft and Mill of Delfrankie are shown in the Valuation Roll of 1884–85, but another entry indicates that part of it had been taken over by the Mains of Glenbucket. Today, the ruined building on the brae is the only sign that it ever existed. There is little doubt that its origin goes back to the days of John Gordon, the fiery Jacobite laird known as Old Glenbuchat. One theory is that it came from *Dail Frangaich,* meaning Frenchman's field, and that it was a name given by a follower of a Strathdon laird who was in France with his master. Another is that the name mean 'Frankie's field'.

Seven miles long, Glenbuchat runs north-west from the River Don to a mountain ridge separating the old counties of Aberdeen and Banff. Hills enclose it on three sides. Once there were clachans the length and breadth of the glen, as there were in other Strathdon glens, but now they are gone. Up to 1850 there were at least seven main settlements in Glenbuchat.

The one enduring link with these forgotten communities is the old whitewashed parish kirk of Glenbuchat, which stands in a secluded corner of the glen under the north shoulder of Ben Newe. It is a plain, unadorned kirk, spartan in its simplicity; as one writer put it, 'a model of primitive but comely decency'. The original church goes back to 1473, but it was rebuilt 1629 and again in 1792. It has remained unaltered since then, although a Laird's Loft was added in 1828. At the end of the 18th century it was covered in heather.

Inside, the walls are plastered, as is the coved ceiling, and the pews on the north and east side of the kirk — old-fashioned box-type pews, some with doors — are set out on three sides of the pulpit. The precentor stands underneath the pulpit, but today his — or her — voice is heard only once a year at an annual service held by 'friends of the church'. Its unvarnished pine furniture and cobbled floor complete a picture that makes it one of the finest examples of a Scottish country kirk to survive from this period.

There is an ornate belfry on the east gable. The bell that it houses carries the date 1643; for over three centuries it summoned glen folk to worship. They came from townships that have long since vanished, or, as change reached out to them, shrunk from six or seven holdings into single units — the farms which today are themselves giving way to change. Their names are perpetuated on the tombstones in the kirkyard, names like Belnaboth, which was first recorded in 1455, or Innerbichate [Inverbuchat], which in 1463 lay untended because the tenant had been executed.

Old, faded stones show the names not only of farming tenants but of merchants, souters and carpenters…people whose skills were essential to the community life of a busy settlement. Among them was Peter Davidson, 'sometime merchant in Belnaboth', who died in 1842. Also at Belnaboth was Peter Young, who died in 1859, aged twenty-two. He was a shoemaker like his father, John Young, who was eighty-two when he died in 1882. At Newton, a short distance from the kirk, there was John Allan, a wright — a vricht — who died in 1625, and a carpenter called John Callam. Most clachans had their tailor. John Kellas was a 'tailor in Glenbucket'. He died in 1832, while Archibald Roger, a tailor at Belnacraig, died in 1849.

There were also gamekeepers. William Brodie was keeper at Backies, up at Glenbuchat Lodge. He died in 1839, and James Brodie, gamekeeper at Drumnagarrie, died nearly half a century later.

Drumnagarrie was obviously Drumnagarrow, whose 'soul-inspiring band' greeted the Earl of Fife when he visited Glenbuchat (see page 19). One of the saddest stones in the kirkyard is that over the grave of Alexander Spencer, who lived at the Mains of Glenbucket and died in 1876. Under his name are the names of his 'dear departed children', who all died in their early years. James in February 1842, aged 6; Elizabeth in May 1848, aged 6; and Peter in May 1846, aged 3.

George Alexander, who lived at the 'Milnetoun of Glenbucket', was listed in the 1696 Poll Tax returns as a 'walker', which probably meant that he worked at a waulk-mill there. On the other hand, a walker or 'wauker' was also a watchman, looking after sheep-folds when the lambs were being weaned. Rannie is a common name in the Glenbuchat kirkyard. The Rannie's were associated with Easter Bucket; two of them died there in the late 19th century. Flat on the ground, its faded letters almost unreadable, is a gravestone recording the death of another Rannie a century earlier — 'Here lyes John Rainy late merchant Easter Bucket died June 4 1767 aged 22'.

Easter Bucket is shown in the 1869 map as a settlement, not simply a farm. Even today, people will tell you about a 'shoppie' that was there at one time and about a 'rickle of steen' where there was a 'hoosie' near the present farmhouse. The present farmer is Bill Thomson, whose family have farmed Easter Bucket for three generations. Up on the brae behind the farmhouse Alistair and Evis Ritchie have a cottage called Culfosie. Like so many place-names, Culfosie has an uncertain origin. Go back three centuries and it becomes Culquhorsie, which in turn came from a common hill name, Quhorsy or Corsky. This meant 'the back of the crossing', which makes sense when you link it with Delfrankie and the old route into the glen.

Stand at Culfosie and look up the long sweep of the glen and there is scarcely a house you will see that isn't occupied by an incomer. Easter Bucket and Blackhillock are the exceptions. Not everyone likes 'white settlers' but they are not a new breed. Near the Water of Carvie is Belnagauld, *Baile nan gall*, the 'town of the strangers or lowlanders'. James Macdonald, in his *Place Names of West Aberdeenshire* in 1899, gave it as 'town of the strangers' — English town'. The 'white settlers' were moving in even then.

Half a mile from Easter Buchat is Culstruphan, the 'corner of the streamlet'. The stream runs between the road and Baltimore farm,

*Rod McGillivray with his grandson at one of the ruined buildings at Belnacraig.*

where there was once a clachan. A road branches off in a long loop by the Mill of Buchat, rejoining the Culstruphan road near Smithyford. Baltimore and Belnacraig lie within the loop, while to the south is Belnaboth. Belnaboth appears on the 1869 map as a fair-sized township, yet the name means 'the town of the huts and bothies', which suggests that at one time there were shielings there.

Modern houses are scattered about the wooded slopes of Belnacraig. I drove up a steep, rough track and found my way blocked by a farm house. 'It's the end of the road', said Rod McGillivray as he came out to meet me. This was Craighead, which Rod and his wife moved into ten years ago. He was working off-shore when I met him, but had plans to retire and make his home in a house that has the most magnificent view in the glen.

The stonework at the gable-end of the building showed where the roof had been raised at the turn of the century. The McGillivrays have retained the atmosphere of the place. Inside, there was a big open fireplace which once boasted a swey. Wallie dogs decorated the mantelpiece and there was a feeling that time had stood still in the old house. It was an impression that was heightened when we went into the garden, for only a few steps away were the foundations of one of the clachan houses; the carter's house, Rob had been told. Beyond that more stonework marked the site of what had been an inn.

Piece by piece, stone by stone, the picture began to come together. Rod took me to the back of the house and up the hill, where the shape of other buildings could be traced out in the grass. One elongated pattern looked as if it might have been a longhouse. Behind them, the line of an old track could be seen, perhaps the road that originally led into the clachan.

From the hill we looked down the glen as far as the eye could see. Rod pointed out Baltimore, just off the Culstruphan road, and he thought there had also been a clachan at Belnaglack. To the north was a long ridge of hills separating Glenbuchat from the Cabrach, with tracks winding their way up to Creag an Sgor and the Garnet Stone. I could see a red-roofed building standing on a high knuckle of ground nearer to us. It was Beltimb, *Bailie tuim,* the town of the knoll, where the old buildings were being restored for use by a religious group.

In 1906 only one thatched house remained in Glenbuchat. It was at Beltimb and it was the last of the old 'cruck framed' cottages in the glen. The couples supporting the roof were sunk deeply into the walls almost to ground level so that the walls themselves bore none of the weight of the roof. This, the last 'thack' in the glen, was demolished to make way for a modern cottage.

I left Craighead and made my way down the hill. The house below Rod's place was occupied by Ken Cruickshank, who was responsible for two photographic books showing Glenbuchat's yesterdays. It was sad to think that the people in them had all gone — and that the people looking at them were mostly incomers.

I travelled round Belnacraig hill and came out at the Smiddyford junction. Less than half a mile beyond it was Netherton, which looks across the Water of Buchat to the Crofts. Last century the Crofts was the home of the Gaulds, a race of giants, famous as fist-fighters, who would have made today's 'heavies' seem puny. The tallest was James Gauld, who was 6 feet 4 inches in height, and the others were only a few inches shorter. It used to be said in Strathdon that anyone under 5 feet 11 inches was a 'sharger' (thin and stunted).

Farther on, two derelict houses stood on either side of a track going over the hills to the Cabrach. One was the deserted farm of Dulax, the other was *Tom na Glais,* shown on some maps as Dulax cottage. The cottage, built in 1865, was a school — Netherton Free Church School — with a roll of 31 pupils, but it closed, following the passing of the Education Act of 1872.

Between the deserted farm and the cottage a rough track ran north towards the Cabrach hills, passing the old croft of Peatfold, which stands picturesquely on the banks of a burn coming down from the moors of Creag an Sgor. In the middle of the 19th century there were five shoemakers and two tailors in this lonely spot. By the turn of the century there was only one souter in the whole glen, supplementing his income by acting as a post-runner.

The Peatfold track joins two other tracks climbing up to Creag an Sgor from Netherton and Upperton. The clachan at Upperton seems to have been superior to most of the old townships. In October, 1868, it was visited by a writer from the *Banffshire Journal,* who described it as 'altogether a treat in the way of old cottages'. Some of the buildings were then over 300 years old. 'The corners are all round outside and inside the houses', the *Journal* noted. 'Many fine convenient wall-presses and even concealments in the walls appear in these curious buildings.'

Today, these 'curious buildings' appeal in a different way, for, threading your way among the ruins, you can still be touched by a sense of what Upperton was like more than a century ago, sprawling along the brae, green fields curving down to the road to Badenyon and, to the north, ancient tracks scrambling up to the flinty head of the Craig of the Sharp Rock. The old farmhouse at Upperton is a shell, but below it a small, red-roofed cottar house is still in use — the last survivor of 'the treat of old cottages' in Glenbucket.

In April, 1902, some thirty years after the *Banffshire Journal's* visit to Upperton, the *Aberdeen Free Press* reported that four or five of the Glenbuchat clachans were still in existence — and still occupied. There were generally seven to ten houses in a clachan, holding 'to the old system when the houses of the inhabitants were huddled together for protection'. The *Free Press* said it was of 'great interest' that they still remained in Glenbuchat, 'the only instance of the kind known to the writer'.

But the day of the clachan was over. James Barclay, MP, who purchased Glenbuchat in 1901, was to rid the glen of these primitive dwellings. When he called at Tullocharrach he found water running out by the front door and was astonished to discover that this seemed normal. At nearby Tarntoul the roof had fallen in and the tenant was living with relatives on a neighbouring farm.

There were, according to Barclay, as many as ten to twenty 'fire-houses' in a clachan, built of stone, lime and clay and with thatched roofs. Peat burned in open fires with large hearths and chimneys sometimes 10 feet wide. The floors were of earth or clay, beaten hard but full of moisture, and the sloping roof gave an impression from the inside of an inverted ship.

James Barclay, the 18th laird of Glenbuchat, was ahead of his time, a landowner who had little in common with the barons and earls who had held the glen since the beginning of the 16th century. Under the Fife lairdship the property was neglected for a century and a half. The Rev Robert Scott, in his report for the New Statistical Account, commented 'The Earl of Fife gives little encouragement here'.

The Fifes were absentee landlords whose policy was to leave the tenants to their own devices. No laird lived in the glen during their tenure. When the Earl of Fife visited his estate in November 1820, it was something of an event. 'Hundreds of people', said the *Aberdeen Journal,* 'turned out to meet him'. Their reward was bread and cheese and 'mountain dew' served up in a tent and a large barn. The surrounding hills blazed with bonfires. 'The rugged Banew [Ben Newe]', said the *Journal,* was one sheet of flame and the Earl 'made every heart bound with joy and every tongue lisp with praise'.

It seemed an unlikely reaction from people who were virtually ignored by their laird, who lived in 'wretched abodes unfit for human habitation', who ate boiled green kale for supper and cauld kale for breakfast the following morning, and whose cattle were so emaciated that they were unable to get up without help. Perhaps it was the mountain dew that did it — or the music. When the earl went to meet his Highlanders he was greeted with a blast of music from 'Drumnagarrow and his soul-inspiring band'. Drumnagarrow is a farm at the foot of Little Firbriggs Hill, north of Easter Buchat. John Strachan, a well-known fiddler who came from the farm, was held in high esteem by Scott Skinner. The Strathspey King was a frequent visitor to Glenbuchat.

Despite its 'soul-inspiring band', the Drumnagarrow farmer seems to have isolated himself from the rest of the community. There is no proper road to the farm; it sits above the glen, hemmed in by fields as if it had been cut adrift from the farms around it. There were two farms there at one time. One farmer was known as Little Drummie,

*This huge kiln, still in good condition, stands on the banks of the Leadensider burn, near the ruined farm of Ryntaing at the head of Glenbuchat. Some idea of its age can be got from the two trees that have grown out of it.*

the other as Muckle Drummie. In recent years, Alan Campbell, a lecturer at Edinburgh University, who lives in the only surviving house in a clachan at Corgarff (*see* Chapter Three), was the occupier at Drumnagarrow. When he moved out his place was taken by Lesley Riddoch, the journalist and broadcaster.

I left Drumnagarrow and went north to Badenyon, which was one of the original clachans in the glen. In one of Ken Cruickshank's books there is a photograph of the site taken in the late 19th century, showing a farm and two crofts. In front of the farmhouse is a shop, but in later photographs it had vanished. Today, the faded 'Badenyon' sign at the roadside covers two buildings — one a

*The ruins of Ryntaing Farm at the head of Glenbuchat.*

deserted farmhouse and its outbuildings, the other an occupied house. Between them a track runs into the moors and at the side of it stones from the 'lost' clachan can be seen.

Between Dulax and Badenyon a track branches off and goes north into the hills by Ballochduie and Newseat. From Newseat a minor track cuts away to the Roch Ford and the Cabrach, passing a ruined farm called the Sluggie. If you stick to the Newseat track you come to another ruined fermtoun, Ryntaing, whose solid stones suggest a fermtoun of some size and importance. There was a water mill there, with a sizeable dam above the farmhouse. The name means 'the point of the tongue', a sharp point of land between the junction of two burns. The burns here are the Leadensider and the Clashwalloch. Clashwalloch means 'the hollow of the pass', but the name Leadensider is more mysterious — it comes from *Leathad ant-saighdear,* 'the hill slope of the soldier'.

On the banks of the Leadensider Burn is a hugh kiln, about 16 feet high and 20 feet broad. You can take a guess at how old it is by looking at the two tall rowan trees that have grown out of the kiln's empty hole. There were a number of kilns in the glen. When I met Mr A C McRobert, from Milton, at Newseat, he told me that the lime stones for the Ryntaing kiln came from a quarry on the west side of Ladylea Hill.

Mr McRobert is a tenant farmer who has a number of farms under

*The school at Balloch — once the most isolated school In Aberdeenshire.*

his wing. Ballochduie, Newseat and ruined Ryntaing among them. Some are let out. He also has Blackhillock, one of the two original farms still being worked in Glenbuchat. He is a Glenbuchat man and went to school at Balloch, south of Badenyon. It was to Balloch that I was going.

The road does a U-turn at Badenyon and runs down to Glen Nochty, passing Glenbuchat Lodge. Half-hidden in the trees on the east side of the road is a small wooden building, abandoned and decaying, its interior stripped bare. This is, or was, Balloch School, single-roomed, and the most isolated school in Aberdeenshire. They used to say it was the school with the biggest playground in Scotland, for behind it stretched an endless expanse of moorland. Now a forest has grown around it, spoiling the joke.

The attendance at the school see-sawed a great deal, depending on the weather and the working demands of the pupils' parents. I was told of a man who, having lost his way, called at Balloch, not knowing it was a school or that the woman there was a teacher. He thought that the youngsters belonged to one family and that Balloch was their home. 'Man!' he was heard to say, 'What a birn o' bairns that woman has!'. But eleven was a small number; in 1868 there were 54 pupils on the roll, learning their lessons in a room that measured 25 feet by 15 feet. The school closed in 1948 with six pupils on the roll.

*Peter Goodfellow in his art gallery at Aldachuie.*

The road to Glen Nochty lies halfway between Glenbuchat Lodge and Bellabeg, where I first saw the sign to Lost. The highest inhabited house in the Glen Nochty is Aldachuie. The first time I saw it, six or seven years ago, it was little different from any other old farmhouse. Peter Goodfellow, a commercial artist, and his wife Jean had settled there and were trying to carve out a living for themselves.

When I went back to Aldachuie in 1996 I found that the old steading by the side of the track had gone. In its place was a modern, glass-fronted gallery, a storehouse of contemporary and modern art, looking almost out of place in this wilderness setting. It was doing well, exhibiting not only Peter's own work but the work of a wide range of professional artists. There was only one possible name for the gallery, and that's what they called it — the Lost Gallery.

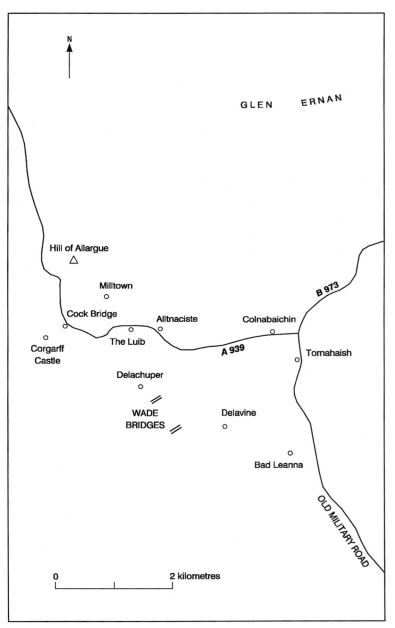

*Map 3. The route from Deeside to Tomintoul by the old military road. The Wade bridges mark the original track to Corgarff and the Lecht.*

## CHAPTER 3

# FEEDING THE CORGARIANS

The crumbling Wade bridges are spaced out along the track like milestones marking the way to Corgarff. All around them the moors are awash with mountain streams. Between Delahaish and Delachuper, a distance of one mile, there are nine fords and four bridges. The streams have names like Caochan Luachair, the rushy streamlet, Allt Bad a' Choilich, burn of the cock's thicket, and Caochan Dubh, the black streamlet. The burn of Delavine, the field or haugh of milk, is a link with the days when cattle droves came this way.

The bridges form part of the old military road from Deeside to Donside, cutting away from the Glaschoille Brae four miles north of the hump-backed Gairnshiel Brig. Near the turn-off there is a piece of hill ground called Bad Leanna. Bad Leanna was 'lying ground', a recognised stance for cattle droves crossing the hill; they were allowed to stay there for 24 hours. Not far down the track at a tiny lochan with the name Ree Newe, the 'shieling of Newe', there was a pen for animals. Remains of an enclosure could be seen there as late as the 1950s.

The use of this corner of Donside as shieling ground for summer grazing was mentioned in *The Donean Tourist*, written in 1828 by Alexander 'Stachie' Laing, an eccentric chapman, 'Tolerably well educated', who was one of the first historians of Donside and Deeside. When I went over the Burn of Tornahaish by the first Wade bridge I was seeing the countryside through Laing's eyes — his 'gley'd' eyes, for he had a squint and was also known as 'Gley'd Sandy'.

Where the Glaschoille joins the Strathdon road at Colnabaichan and runs on to Cock Bridge there are frequent reminders of communities that have shrunk or vanished since 'Gley'd Sandy' tramped the Donside moors with his pack on his back. 'Dorna Haisch' or Tornahaish, is no longer a hamlet; Colnabaichan, described a century ago as 'a struggling hamlet', now lives on only as a farm; the chapels at Corriehoul and Ordacoy have long since gone, and as you go west you half-expect to hear the ring of a hammer on an anvil as you pass the house where Jane Seymour lives.

*One of the old Wade bridges on the military road to Corgaff Castle.*

She was born at Roadside. Her grandfather, Sandy Grant, was blacksmith there for sixty years, and her father, Charles Grant, followed him. He died in 1936 and the smiddy closed in 1938.

Wullie Gray at the Luib once told me the story of a tight-fisted farmer who fed his horses so poorly that they were skin and bones. He sent one to Sandy Grant at the Roadside smiddy to be shoe'd and when a neighbour saw him with the horse he asked what he was doing. 'Ach!' said Sandy, 'I'm makin' a horse.' 'Fit dae ye mean, "making" a horse?', said his neighbour. 'Well!', said Sandy, 'Niven sent me the frame an' I'm fillin' it in.'

I was looking for the Street. Not far from Corgarff, near the old post office at Greenbank, a distinctive cottage with a ruined steading at its gable-end can be seen a short distance from the road. Its black and white walls set it apart from other houses; its name is Alltnaciste, which means the 'burn of the kist or hollow'. It is the last remaining building in a row of houses once known as the Street. The burn that gave it its name is farther on, coming down to the Don on the line of a track reaching back through the hills by the Moss of Allt na Ciste to Glen Ernan.

The house at Alltnaciste was in poor condition when Alan Tomain Campbell, a lecturer in anthropology at Edinburgh University, moved into it. His mother taught for a time at Corgarff School, as did his

*Alan Campbell at Alltnaciste.*

grandmother. He was born at Alltnaciste…'through in that room,' he indicated…and as we sat and talked about the old clachan and the wild, lonely country around it it became clear that he had been caught up in its magic. His brother, a teacher in Edinburgh, had a house in Tornahaish, where there was formerly a hamlet and an inn.

Outside, we stamped on the grass and felt the foundations of two of the 'lost' clachan buildings under our feet. There had been shiels in the area too, for Alan had come upon the ruins of one on the banks of the Alltnaciste burn, and the remains of what appeared to be shiels could be seen near a number of other burns. Apart from Alltnaciste, there were only two buildings in the Street still traceable, but an old map of Strathdon showed that there had been a number of houses; enough, at anyrate, to justify the title of 'Street'.

The word 'Street' was often used to denote a row of houses or crofts. A former row of houses at Loinahaun, west of Gairnshiel, and another row south of Abergeldie, were known simply as The Street. It sometimes appeared in Gaelic, as in Sraid Mhoine Ailttridh, the Street of Monaltrie, south of Balnaut on the old road near Cairnequheen.

When I first met Alan Campbell he had just returned from a two-year stay in Brazil, where he had been living in the Amazon forest with a people called the Wayapi. He had been studying the Wayapi

Indians since 1974 and was the author of a number of books, including *Getting to know Waiwai,* an Amazonian ethnography. Waiwai was the chief of the Wayapi.

So we were both involved in a search for communities that had vanished or, in his case, were in danger of vanishing. I was looking for a 'lost' world of clachans and shielings, trying to discover something about the people who had lived in them, while he was learning about a faraway race threatened with 'the violence of invasion' and eventual destruction. The taking of the Wayapi lands, the clearing of the forests for logging profit, held echoes of the Highland Clearances, and it was not surprising that the Scottish hills were often in Alan's thoughts. When the Amazonian winds went 'berserk' he would recall 'the wildness of the weather at home, its fierce unpredictability, its constant changes'. At moments like that he would feel pangs of homesickness He would remember lines from Stevenson's *Blows the wind today,* with its standing stones on a wine-red moor, sheep on the hills — and the howes of the silent vanished races.

When we were studying old 1869 and 1902 maps, Alan pointed out a large forest that had virtually disappeared by the time the second had been printed. Later, a passage in his book brought this to mind again. The loss of a forest, he wrote, was 'like a bereavement'. He remembered sitting by some ruins, 'a shieling most likely from a time when Gaelic was spoken in these areas', looking down on the remains of the old Caledonian Forest. 'So little of it was left there; just a defiant band of pine trees, gloomy and dark, straggling across the hillside, hunched against the wind, looking over their shoulders at the empty slopes all round them.'

He wrote, too, about the way humans treat animals — 'destroying animals and birds for fun is more and more being recognised as an unacceptable activity.' Scotland he said, had a particularly acute problem in that most of the Highlands was owned by 'rich toffs'. He saw them through Hugh MacDiarmid's eyes, quoting lines from his 'Island Funeral':

> Red-faced, merely physical people
> Whose only thought looking over
> These incomparable landscapes
> Is what sport they will yield
> How many deer and grouse.

I thought about the locked gates I had seen closing in the sprawling acres of the Cabrach, and about other lairds who had grudgingly allowed hillwalkers on to their estates, or attempted by more subtle means to keep them out. I thought, too, about the Royal estate at Delnadamph, which I was heading for after leaving Corgarff. I had been talking with Alan Campbell about how the lodge there had been demolished and buried. As MacDiarmid's verses had said, all they wanted to know was what sport it would yield, how many deer and grouse.

When Alexander Laing crossed the Don after passing Alltnaciste he came to 'a small current, by a stone bridge, where the military road intersects the ravine'. This stone bridge was the last of the three Wade bridges on the stretch of moorland between Bad Leanna and the Cock Bridge road. Today it is a frail arc barely wide enough or strong enough to take anyone over the Allt Damh, the Ox-burn, which Laing called the Aldn Dow. That is how it is still pronounced.

The place-name expert, James Macdonald, said there was a farm beside the burn called Aldamph, a corruption of Allt Damh. The 1869 Ordnance Survey map shows Aldamph as a number of ruined buildings in a field next to Delachuper, which sits on the edge of the track a short distance west of the bridge. The last house on the military road is Ordgarff. In 1676, records mentioned a place near here as 'ye Lyb more of Corgarff', and there are accounts of cattle being driven to an inn at Lybmore during the shieling months last century.

Lybmore was the Luib, where the Bard of Corgarff lives today. Wullie Gray is known to hundreds of visitors to the Lonach Gathering. He is the man seen leading a horse and cart in the wake of the Men of Lonach when they march to the Games after calling at the houses of the local lairds. Toasts are made, whisky drunk, and Wullie's cairtie is there in case anyone falls by the wayside. No prostrate bodies have ever been seen on it yet, as far as I know, but if that did happen the Bard would probably write a poem about it.

Wullie's sheep farm lies near the Luib Bridge, where the Alltnaciste Burn joins the Don, His 'beat' covers 30,000 acres stretching north to the Lecht ski slopes and across bleak moorland to the Braes of Glenlivet. His poems have often told about his work, 'diggin' for neeps, muckin' the byre, takin' in peat tae stoke the fire, feedin' the hens, milkin' the coos, and sortin' the feet o' cripplin' ewes'.

I had come down the old military road in the footsteps of Ensign Rutherford, of General Pulteney's Regiment, which was stationed at Corgarff Castle. I was heading for an old township mentioned in the Ensign's description of the Corgarff area — 'After crossing the River don, about half a Mile below Corgarff, the road passes through a Village call'd Miln Town of Allairg, afterwards over a High Mountain call'd Lecht, falls down and crosses the Burn of Lecht.'

So this old clachan was a vital communications link in the uneasy years following the '45 Jacobite Rising. The approach to it from the Corgarff road today is by a rough track to the east of the Luib. It stands on either side of the Milltown Burn, which comes down from Coire Riabhach, overlooking the Lecht. When I was standing with Wullie Gray on the bridge over the burn he quoted a poem he had written about it:

> This is the water
> That drove the wheel
> To mak' the meal
> To feed the Corgarians

The River Don takes a great loop below the Milltown, giving weight to the Luib's Gaelic meaning, the 'bend of a stream'. It runs past a wooded hillock called Tom na Dubh-bhruaich (pronounced Tam doobrach), the Hillock of the Black Brae. This may be a reference to how it looked before the land was afforested. When Wullie Gray came to the Luib thirty years ago there were no trees; the whole area was under cultivation.

The old meal mill, now used as a store, still stands on the route going through Milltown to the Lecht. Wullie pointed out the ruins of the miller's house higher up the Milltown Burn. There was a ruined croft still farther up; the crofter, Wullie said, had also worked in Allargue. The White House up on the hill was Auchmore, a listed building.

'That', said Wullie, pointing to a heap of rubble, 'was the sweetie shoppie and that', pointing to a mound of stones, 'was the cobbler's shop'. These dead stones tell you little about the Milltown, but you can walk through the door of an old cottage known as the Bothie and find yourself taking a step back in Donside's history. The Bothie is used by Wullie — and it is exactly as it has been for as far back as Corgarff folk can remember.

The Bothie is divided into three sections. The middle section was where the peats were stored and the dogs kept. A rough wooden ladder takes you up to the loft, which is above the living quarters

*Willie Gray outside the Bothie at Milntown of Allargue.*

(Wullie uses this room as a store). On the right another door leads through to what was a combined stable and byre, the horse on one side, the cow in its stall on the other side.

A faded page from an old newspaper was stuck on the wall of the peat room. I could barely read the advertisements on it. Wullie told me a tale about this tattered piece of newsprint...about what happened the day a man came to the Bothie selling peats. 'He had this fairmer wi him fae Glenlivet', said Wullie, 'an' I said till him, "Fit wis ye dae'n in '45?" He says, "I jist couldna tell ye that." I said, "Ye wis advertisin' for a horseman, somebody tae ca' a pair o' horse".'

The farmer stood looking at him with his mouth open, thinking that here was a man could see into someone's past, never mind his future. But there was a simple explanation. When Wullie heard the man's name and was told he came from Glenlivet he remembered seeing an advertisement from the farmer in the paper on the wall. It stuck in his mind over the years...until the farmer who wanted someone to 'ca' a pair o' horse' walked through the Bothie door.

Wullie pointed out an almost unreadable scribble pencilled on the stable door. It read, 'Horse badly lamed'. The date was the 9th of July, 1945. Below it another indistinct scrawl read, 'Bad day'. Using barn doors to record events was a common practice at one time. Wullie showed me other markings on the Bothie door. The letters

GM were there — the initials of George Morrison, an earlier Bothie resident. The number could also be seen. Wullie was looking for the initials AS, for these were on the end of a branding iron which he still keeps in the bothy. They were the initials of a flockmaster called Stewart. The branding irons were tested on the door, burned into the woodwork before being used on the animals.

In the room where the peat was stored a roughly made ladder led up to the loft where the shepherd slept. The wool was stored in the loft. A rope still dangled from a coupling. When the wool was being taken away sacks were hung from the rope and the wool loaded into them. From the peat room, a door opened into the shepherd's living quarters. An old mangle stood there. Through a door on the right was the gable-end room where the horse and cattle were kept.

On the wall of the peat room hung two pairs of sheep shears. Outside were the sheepfolds. I once saw him shearing sheep there with hand shears, perpetuating a craft that has long since given way to more modern methods. Wullie sticks to the old way, partly because by cutting by hand he can layer the wool so that water runs off the sheep's back instead of soaking into it, and partly because he is at home with the old way. A shears to Wullie is what a last is to a souter.

He has proved over the years that few shepherds can beat him in this old skill. When he first came to the Luib he had only a small piece of ground, so to give himself a liveable income he travelled the country shearing sheep from May till August. He sheared about 200 a day — 13,000 a year. Now he shears 600 a week on the Luib — 100 a day. He has 1,100 sheep on the farm.

Wullie was asked to take part in the Grampian TV programme 'Walking Back to Happiness'. Eileen Macallum, who presented the programme, asked him if he was content with his lot. Wullie's reply was direct but none the less telling. He said wryly that he certainly wasn't working there for the money. But his attitude to life in a part of the country which can become Arctic-like in winter is shown in one of his poems:

> The cald north wind, a frost see hard,
> Strathdon is like a Christmas card,
> Though peniless if you live there
> You're richer than a millionaire.

I left Wullie and the Luib, crossed the Milltown water and climbed up the Hill of Allargue, picking up an old track called the Green Road, keeping clear of an area by the Milltown Burn known as the Fleuchats. The name comes from *fliuch,* meaning a wet place. Great wastes of moorland stretched in front of me. I was heading for another track that reached into the hills…to Inchrory and the shieling lands of Strathavon.

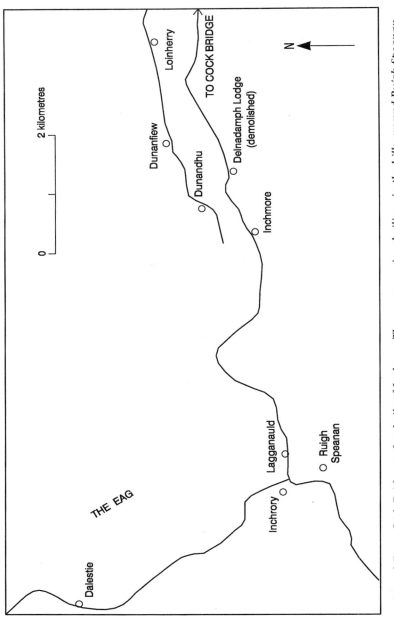

*Map 4. From Cock Bridge to the sheils of Inchrory. There were major sheilings in the hills around Ruigh Speanan.*

# CHAPTER 4
# THE SHIELINGS

The old road running west from Cock Bridge, shying away from the fearsome Lecht Pass, has had its share of travellers through the centuries — drovers pushing their cattle through the hills to markets in the south…Queen Victoria riding over it on a pony called 'Victoria' and marvelling at the 'enchanting hills'…soldiers scouring the glens for 'barbarous thieving Highlanders'…and the cateran, 'broken hielandmen and sorners', raging down from Badenoch to plunder and ravage the countryside. They brought, it was said, 'insufferable evil' on the land.

It was this road, 'thinly inhabited' in those far-off days, that I took when I went in search of a 'lost' land of shiels and bothies. Behind me, traffic grumbled over the Lecht on its way to Tomintoul, but the world it belonged to faded away as I went west, past the fields where sheep grazed, past the larachs and farms, on by Inchmore, the most westerly house on Donside, and through moorland that seemed to stretch away to the very rim of the world.

The road from Corgarff to Inchrory has changed little in two and a half centuries. There is a scattering of holdings on the north side of the Don — 'the last evidences of successful struggling with nature in Corgarff', wrote Alex Inkson McConnachie in 1901. For some the struggle has long since ended. Delnadamph Lodge was at one time the only house of any size on the south side of the Don. Now it, too, has gone. The lodge, originally a croft, stood in a lovely setting beside a small lochan, fringed with trees. It was bought by the Queen for Prince Charles, but it was later demolished. Secretly it seemed, for it was there one day and gone the next. Hillwalkers heading for Inchrory found to their surprise that there was an empty site and no lochan. The stones from the lodge lay at the bottom of the pond, which was filled in and smoothed over as if Delnadamph had never existed.

Tramping down the dusty miles to Inchrory, I was walking in the footsteps of Redcoats who had marched out from Corgarff Castle in the bitter aftermath of the '45 Rising, on patrol and on the lookout for rebels wearing the proscribed tartan. They detested

*Delnadamph.*

this bleak, unfriendly land. It was hemmed in by mountains and 'full of boggs'. It was 'the most Dismal Country as I ever saw', wrote an unhappy Captain Edhouse, who was in charge of the Braemar barracks. He said they would have fared better 'if the Inhabitants were not up in their Sheilings, some five or six miles amongst the Hills'.

His report was dated 3 June, 1750. It was shieling time, the month in which the old passes were caught up in a great tide of movement, men, women and children heading out into the hills as if on some Biblical exodus. Geographers called it transhumance — the seasonal migration of livestock to summer grazing. For centuries, people had moved their cattle and sheep from their lowland pastures to the high glens so that they could feed on the rich fibrous hill grasses during the summer months. They were there from June till September, and in that time their cattle fattened and the grassland in their winter quarters was rested.

The annual migration of cattle to the upland shielings for summer grazing goes a long way back. In the 17th century it expanded because of a considerable increase in the sale of black cattle to England; it was said that Scotland had become 'a mere grazing field to England'.

# THE SHIELINGS

An 'Account of the Shire of Forfar' in 1654–85 said that in the summer the folk of Glenisla 'goe to the far distant Glens which border upon Braemar and they live, grassing their cattle in little houses, which they build upon their coming and throw down when they come away, called sheels. Their diet is only milk and whey and what venison or wylld foull they can apprehend.' The 'little houses' were small circular huts made of turf. They were known as beehive huts. It was probably these that Thomas Pennant, the naturalist and traveller, saw when travelling through Scotland in 1744. He thought they were 'shocking to humanity, formed of loose stones and covered with clods, which they called divots, or with heath, broom or branches of fir'. They looked, he said, 'like so many black mole-hills'.

From Corgarff the summer grazings spread along the Don to Inchrory, up the banks of Meoir Veannaich, and on the grassy haughs of the River Avon by Glenmullie and the Conglass Water. The Inchrory road runs through ground that was once said to be 'mossy, and scarce passable'. On the high ground on the south side of the road, on the Aberdeenshire–Banffshire boundary, the Allt an Mhicheil, Michael's Burn, spills from the Well of Don and goes eastward to join a jumble of other headstreams as the River Don. Near Inchmore, on the north side of the track, a little used hill road swings away to Tomintoul by the Eag. 'Eag' is a Gaelic word for a notch or cleft and this can be seen clearly on the skyline from Delnadamph.

There is a bothy at Inchmore used by hillwalkers. On the opposite side of the track the sparse remains of a cottage can be seen on a knoll topped by two trees. Black Jenny McHardy lived there. They say you could hardly see the inside of her house for peat smoke, so it isn't difficult to guess how she got her nickname. Outside, all that remains is a sheepfold. Jimmy Shiach, who knew Black Jenny, was a shepherd at Corgarff — the last shepherd to stay at Inchmore, where there was once a shieling.

Jimmy was the Auchmair farmer I met in the Cabrach (see Chapter One). He remembers keeping hens at Inchmore; they laid nearly every day, he says, all the year round, and he 'made some cash from them'. That was back in 1949–50 when eggs were 4/- a dozen. His 'beat' was from Inchmore up to Inchrory and 'roon by the Broon Coo'. This was the Brown Cow Hill, between Corgarff and Glen Gairn, which Queen Victoria passed on her way through the hills in

*Inchmore Bothy in winter.*

1859.A large snow-drift which often lingers there until midsummer is known locally as the Brown Cow's White Calf.

Jimmy also went 'up by the Feith', north of the road from Corgarff. 'Oot at Feith afore ye see Inchrory there's een o' those health wells there. I hinna been up since they made the hill roads. I was awa' by then.' Jimmy was talking about the Feith Bhait, a stream running through grazings at the head of the Don. Today, the area is known as the Faevait, or simply the Fae, and the sulphurous well is called the Fae Well. The land here was important shieling territory, spreading out from the old hill route by the Eag.

I was looking for Ruigh Speanan, which was once described as 'a situation unequalled among the shearing places of the parish'. It can first be seen where the road from Corgarff turns south towards Inchrory, a broad shoulder of grassland high above the A'an. From the main route a track turns off and climbs up and around the hill. To get to the edge of Ruighe Speanen you have to cut across the moor to where a large weather-vane has been erected. As you approach it the heather gives way to grassland, part of the grazing territory of the shieling.

'Stachie' Laing's meaning of Ruigh Speanan — 'ruah-spinen' was how he spelt it — was 'the place where lambs are weaned'. James

Macdonald gave it the name shown in the 1869 Ordnance Survey map — Ruigh Spairne, the 'slope of the contest or hard struggle'. This definition seems the most likely one. The main grazing area is a broad ledge of pasture backed by rough cliff, and it is here that there are traces, barely visible, of shieling buildings. The remains of small, circular structures, probably used as storage places, lie close to the rocks. In front, facing up Glenavon, were four large shiels, 14 feet to 18 feet broad.

There can be few shieling sites as spectacular as Ruighe Speanan. It is one of Nature's grandstands, a place where you can sit God-like above the land and survey the world below with a sense of awe. Down there a breathtaking panorama opens up as the River Avon slips past Inchrory House and swings north to Tomintoul. To the west it reaches far back to Loch A'an, a thin sliver of light cutting through the dark mass of the Glen Avon hills. Seven miles up that lonely glen was Faindouran Lodge, now a bothy. There were shieling places called the Bothan Dubh near Faindouran.

The great peaks of the Cairngorms lie across the river from Ruigh Speanan...Ben A'an, Ben A'Bhuird, Cairngorm and distant Ben Macdhui. I crossed the plateau and looked down Glen Builg. The hill slopes of Meall Gaineimh on the west side of the Builg Burn were where the Redcoats had their military posts, watching out for the plundering cateran, and on the opposite side of the burn were green pastures where shiels were built between Inchrory and Loch Builg.

'In former times every glen had its crofts and shielings', wrote Seton Gordon, 'now even the ruins may not be found without careful search'. That was more than seventy years ago and today it is even more difficult, so that the story of the shiels, the tales that were told in them, the songs that were sung, are drifting out of our ken. Yet every shiel *did* have its story. There was Ruigh Bristidh Cridhe, the Shieling of the Broken Heart. What sad tale lay behind that name? There was also Ruigh Caillich, the Old Woman's Shieling, and near Lochan Uaine in Glenmore are the ruins of Ruigh da Ros, the Shieling of the Two Promontories. Behind that odd title lay the story of an old man who put a curse on a woman who came to him for help, so that she fled from his door blinded.

Seton Gordon thought that Meur na Banaraiche, the Dairymaid's Finger, near Loch A'an, had a link with the shielings. It was probably a relic of the time when people went up the A'an to the loch for the summer grazing, and the shieling where the dairymaid lived may have been at the foot of the stream. That, at anyrate, was Gordon's theory. Sitting up there on Ruigh Speanan, I wondered what tales had been spun about the folk who had come to this lofty shieling. They were from St Bridget and Tomintoul, part of the great caravan of men, women *and* children that migrated down the A'an to Inchrory and Loch Builg and even east to Corgarff for the summer grazing.

Shieling life on Ruigh Speanan would have been little different from life in countless other shiels scattered about the Cairngorms. Away to the west of Inchrory, beyond Loch A'an and great scar of the Lairig Ghru, is Glen Einich. It was there that Colonel Thomas Thornton, traveller, sportsman and *bon viveur,* made camp during his Sporting Tour in 1804. At Sgoran Dubh, high above Loch Einich, the Colonel and his party sat 'on the brink of that frightful precipice' and had a lavish picnic lunch.

Down at Loch Einich they saw small herds of cattle grazing on the pastures at the loch and came upon a lone bothy, 'the temporary residence of a lonely herdsman'. They discovered that the herd's fare was a good deal more frugal than their own — 'oatcakes, butter or cheese and often the coagulated blood of their cattle spread on their bannocks'. Thornton gave a detailed description of life in 'a boothee or sheelin'. It was, he said, 'the dairy house where the highland shepherds live with their herds and flocks and during the fine seasons make butter and cheese and gather juniper berries which they sell for a good price'.

'Their whole furniture', he went on, 'consists of a few horn spoons, their milking utensils, a couch formed of sods to lie on, and a rug to cover them'. There was no champagne for them; instead, they drank 'milk, whey, and sometimes by way of indulgence, whisky'.

The sight of a lone herdsman was unusual. Generally, whole families went to the hills during the transhumance season. Youngsters became herdsmen when they were in their teens, and before that were given 'cabers' to drive off stray cattle. They learned to build and repair shiels, and sometimes to poach, while the girls helped the dairymaids and were taught to knit and spin by their mothers.

The time of the shieling was given an almost idyllic air in Gaelic verse and song. The men were seen basking in the sun or lounging in the whisky house, while the women enjoyed their temporary escape from the drudgery of their daily darg on the crofts. Duncan

Campbell, editor of the *Northern Chronicle* in 1896, read a paper to the Inverness Scientific Society about life in the shielings.

'The ruins of their huts and folds were like deserted villages when I first remember them', he wrote, 'I lived amongst those who were brought up in the disused shielings and from the age of nine to thirteen had a boy's experience of shieling life myself between the years 1837 and 1841'. Although he was seeing shieling life in its last stages it retained 'a weird hold' on him all his days.

'The spirit of the hills seemed to lay a spell upon us', he said. He was caught up in a world of thunder and storm, roaring streams in flood, and whirling mists. 'The eerie feelings came in the still nights when the dogs sat on their haunches to howl at nothing visible, and when the faint voices of the small rivulets, nearly dried up in summer heats, made a ghostly melody.'

But however idyllic it may have seemed, the real reason for their annual migration was always in the background, as could be seen in a dialogue song about a woman looking forward to her temporary release from the monotony of life on the croft. Francis Diack, the Celtic linguist from Aberdeen, quoted in his *Inscriptions in Pictland* the thoughts of a couple before they moved to their ruigh — shieling — in the hills: *Nan tigeadh an sambr', Ach (am) faireadh sinn chun 'in ruigh.*

> She.  When the summer comes
> And we go to the shieling,
> I'll get away from your scolding
> And we'll have a quiet time for once.
>
> He.  But when the summer comes
> It will not be a time for idleness,
> But for getting busy with wool and tartan
> And getting the weaving put in order.

From Ruighe Speanan I could see the track from Corgarff winding down to Inchrory, passing Lagganauld, where Queen Victoria 'lunched in a splendid position' before going on 'by the so-called "Brown Cow"'. The stones from dykes across the road from Lagganauld are said to have been used in the building of shielings. Beyond this were the steep cliffs of Cait nan Gabhar and the slopes of Carn Bad a' Ghuail. The rocky hill slopes on the approach to Inchrory from the north were unsuitable for grazing, but there was good shieling land higher up. There were six or seven bothies on these plateaus. The best and busiest shieling area was the Favait.

The Fae was enclosed by the ridges of Carn Bad a' Ghual and Ruigh Speanan on the west and Craig Veann and Culchaviee on the east. The ridges formed a green bowl 600 feet deep, the rim rising to 2,300 feet. There were more than twenty bothies in the Faevait at one time. Droving traffic from the north came through the Fae, leaving the A'an near Dalestie and following the Burn of Little Fergie to the lower slopes of Craig Veann and over the Eag to Inchmore.

The shielings in the Faevait are shown on a map by William Anderson dated 1770. The 'Old Shilling call'd Campbell's Rive' was near the Strathdon road and a short distance away were 'Bothies call'd the Inver of the Clachan Dow'. A note beside the Hill of Culchary said, 'Good pasture along the face of this Hill partly Grass and partly Heath. Not over wet'. John Gordon, the fiery 'Old Glenbucket' of Jacobite fame, had grazing in the Favait at the 'Stance of Glenbukets Bothie'. The 'Strone of Clash Yarich' was Culsharrach, or Strone ma Crois-Arach, where the road to Inchrory goes through a nose-shaped bend three miles west of Delnadamph.

Written across the map are the words 'Controverted ground called the Fae Vait'. There was a long-running dispute between the tenants of Strathavon and Corgarff over the shieling boundaries.

It was down the long corridor of the A'an that the cateran came. Shielings were frequently the target of 'broken hielandmen' from Badenoch and Lochaber, armed with bows, quivers, swords, gauntlets and platesleeves. One report in July, 1609, told of a raid on Lord Elphinstone's 'scheils' in the lands of Corgarff, when his lordship's bowmen were assaulted, bound and left for dead. Twelve sheep and four 'nott' (cows) were driven off.

I went to Tomintoul to follow the reivers' trail, down the A'an by the bridges of Delnabo and Delavorar, chasing ghosts along a river where birch trees bow over 'the clearest and purest waters of all our kingdom'. In a sense my search started at the keeper's house at Birchfield, where a gate shuts out traffic but lets walkers through. Graeme Ormirod, assistant keeper on the Glenavon estate, was there. When I asked him about the shiels he said, 'They're all over the place'. He was right. On the green haughs across the A'an and on the plateaus high above the river ruined shielings marked my route all the way to Inchrory.

Keepers do their job efficiently nowadays, sometimes at the expense of goodwill, but I doubt if any could be as unpopular as Robert Willox, who was the Duke of Gordon's deer forester in Glenavon from 1762 to 1794. He lived at Wester Gaulrig, which is about half a mile south of Birchfield on the west side of the A'an. An incomer, Willox was detested by local folk; he once said that when anyone was attached to the Duke 'the whole peopell is against him'.

There was a poindfold (an enclosure for impounding stray cattle and horses) at Wester Gaulrig and Willox's over-zealous use of it won him many enemies. He was well aware of what would happen if he ran into some of then 'in a driftie night'. Beside the gate at Birchfield a track climbs up to Achnahyle, opening up a fine view of the river.

Beyond Achnahyle the Muckle Fergie Burn comes tumbling into the A'an. One of its tributaries, Meur an Loin, was shieling country but now red deer roam the hill where cattle once grazed. Beyond Torbain, I saw deer silhouetted against the sky on a ridge of Carn Dubh. Down by the river, where it keeps company with the road as it loops round to Dalestie, the Burn of Little Fergie comes in from the east, crossing the old drove road of the Eag More, which pushed through the Faevait to Inchmore.

On the last stretch of the A'an from Little Fergie to Inchrory there are signs of shielings on both sides of the river, some of them shown on present-day maps. On the right (east) bank they can be seen at Fail an Tuirc, on the green haughs of Dail an Sac, and on Dail Neilead. On the west bank there were shielings by a small lochan at Elanguish. They are out of sight from the Inchrory road, but the lochan can be seen from the rocky defile where the Caochan Searrach burn comes down. This burn is shown on the 1869 six-inch OS map as Jessie's Burn.

The crags and scree slopes of the Neilad limited the amount of pasturing on the approaches to Inchrory, but up on top the grazings spread out on undulating slopes at a height of 2,000 feet. Below them the A'an takes another great loop near the Lochan Eileaan a' Ghiuthais and a little farther on the track from Tomintoul ends its eight-mile run to Inchrory.

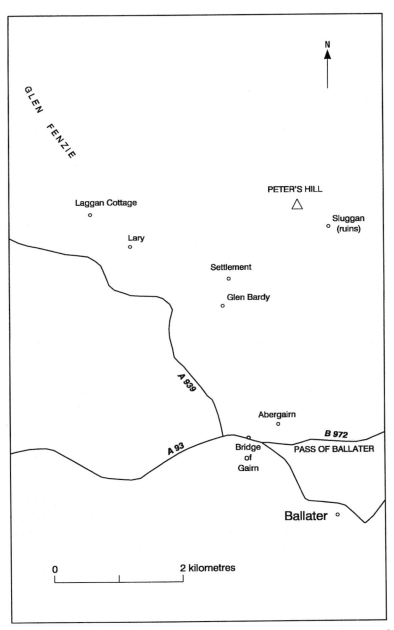

*Map 5. The Land of Gairn — from the Bridge of Gairn to Lary and Laggan, taking in ruins in Glen Bardy and the Sluggan.*

# CHAPTER 5
# LAND OF GAIRN

The Land of Gairn spreads out from the great granite tors of Ben A'an to Byron's 'Morven of Snow'. It gives its name to the River Gairn, the longest tributary of the Dee, rising in the corrie of Eag Dubh and pushing its way east fed by turbulent burns with names like the Big Essie, the Allt Phouple, the Muckle Licherie and the Pitomie. There were shiels on the Big Essie and at the foot of Pitomie at one time. It passes the Bealach Dearg, the old Red Pass to Tomintoul, crosses the military road from Crathie to Gairnshiel, and ends its 20-mile journey at the Fit o' Gairn.

It was from there that I began my journey up Gairnside. Two well-used roads run north from the Fit o' Gairn, hugging the river on either side until it swings away to the west below Lary. One road follows it to Gairnshiel, where it links up with the Crathie road to form a loop to Deeside, while the second road — a commutation road — peters out on the opposite side of the water at Lary Farm. But there is another, near-forgotten road which some say was once the main route into the glen.

This third road follows the line of a track which runs from the Pass of Ballater to Abergairn Farm. The track passes the front door of the house where Ian and Margaret Cameron live almost on top of an old lead mine. On the brae behind the house there is a long ridge where the main shaft of the mine was sunk. Tunnels were made to take out the rock and the exit of one can be seen in a field below the house.

Not far from the farm is all that is left of the clachan of Upper and Lower Corrybeg. The 1869 Name Books* said there were a number of small houses in Upper Corrybeg, two of which were used as dwelling houses and as a grocer's shop, another as 'offices' (farm buildings). The houses, which were straw thatched and 'in middling repair', extended on each side of the Corrybeg Burn. At Lower Corrybeg there were three thatched dwelling houses, several small 'offices', all thatched and in bad repair, and a small farm steading.

*Name Books provided information about places in the six-inch Ordnance Survey map of 1869.

By 1921, Corrybeg had virtually disappeared. In that year, G M Fraser wrote in *The Old Deeside Road* that Corrybeg was 'a lively neighbourhood hamlet within living memory, but now entirely out of existence'. As the old people died off the cottages were demolished and the ruins covered up. 'Only the stone walls that enclosed the gardens are now to be seen at Corrybeg', said Fraser. I came to Corrybeg when old Scots roses were blooming in those abandoned gardens, just as they had done a century ago. It was a bouquet from the past.

Ian Cameron has an old estate map which carries the names of some of Corrybeg's residents. Women feature prominently in it...Mrs Coutts at Dikehead Cottage in Lower Corrybeg, Mrs Forbes in Upper Corrybeg, and Mrs Stewart at the Prony. Looking at it, I wanted to reach into the past to learn something about them, who they were, what they did, whether they were sad or happy. I wondered about the lives they had led in this tiny clachan — *Coire beag,* the little corrie. I wondered, too, about Meg Morris of Corrybeg and where she had lived, for I had heard that she was the glen's unofficial physician...'the doctor for a'body on Gairnside', it was said, 'gathering herbs and healing scurvies and onything o' that kind'.

Beyond Corrybeg another track breaks away and climbs through a birch wood skirting the Craig of Prony. From the top of the brae the river can be seen wriggling its way to the Fit o' Gairn, passing Candacraig, where the last Roman Catholic chapel in the glen once stood. Farther on is the farm of Lary. But I was going another way, round the scree-riddled slopes of the Craig of Prony and down into Glen Bardy...into a 'lost' world known only to hillwalkers, grouse-shooters and shepherds. I met one of them coming down from the glen with his two dogs — young Calum Wright, who works as a shepherd on his father's farm at the Prony. They have 250 sheep to look after and Calum was out checking on them.

The track dropped sharply down to the Glenbardy Burn, where stepping stones took me across a small ford and up to Glen Bardy croft. The ruined buildings and the long dykes seemed to indicate other holdings in this little glen. William M Alexander, in his *Place Names of Aberdeenshire,* said there were the remains of an old settlement there. Surveys have since given indications of long-houses and enclosures.

Looking back the way I had come I was awe-struck by what I saw. The great mass of Lochnagar filled the skyline, its corries black against late winter snow, clouds swirling and dancing in the gullies. The sun broke through, turning the downhill track into a long finger of gold, softening the harsh face of the Craig of Prony. I doubt if there is a more magnificent view of Lochnagar anywhere else on Deeside.

It heightened the sense of isolation in this hidden glen, where the broken remains of buildings lay across the brae like pieces of a discarded jigsaw. It was certainly a 'lost' valley, reminding me of the Lost Valley of Bidean nam Bian in Glencoe, where the Macdonalds sheltered from the murderous Campbells, and where stolen cattle were hidden away when clansmen came back from their raids. I wondered if Morven Jamie had ever driven his stolen beasts into Glenbardy. His real name was James Coutts and he was the last of the Deeside cateran, selling his stolen cattle to unscrupulous dealers taking their droves to markets in the south. When the net closed in on him he took ship from Aberdeen for India, 'I'm awa', but where I'll go and what I'll dee I little ken,' he said, 'but the bonnie braes o' Morven I'll see nae mair.'

I left the glen and followed a track that climbed out of Glenbardy and went east to Peter's Hill, where it met another track coming up from Balmenach. I could see a party of hillwalkers plodding up from Balmenach on their way to Morven. Beyond them a large area of open grassland lay on the south side of Peter Hill and it was there that I found the remains of a settlement above the Sluggan Burn. The word *slugan* means 'gullet', and here the 'gullet' was taking the Sluggan water to the Tullich Burn. The ruins were substantial. The outline of gardens could be seen in front of them. The fields stretching away from them were known as the Sluggan parks and along the edge of these a narrow path led to the croft of Easter Morven, where a derelict shepherd's house stood above the Tullich Burn.

When you walk 'the bonnie braes o' Morven' by the Culsten and Tullich Burns you are more than likely to come upon the remains of old shiels and deserted settlements…longhouses and enclosures, cairns and field systems, and maybe even the hint of an old whisky still. Ian Shepherd, Aberdeenshire Council's archaeologist, came across what was thought to be a whisky still in 'a very secluded spot' near the Culsten Burn. Coming to Morven from the west by Glenfenzie you pass the remains of a depopulated settlement on the Glac Road, an old track from Glen Fenzie farm to Wester Morven.

*The settlement above the Sluggan Burn.*

It is officially classed as a 'township'. Just to the north of the farm another 'township' can be seen at the side of a track running to the foot of Sron Gharbh. Here, there were at least seven longhouses and enclosures.

Cuthbert Graham's Portrait of *Aberdeen and Deeside,* carried a poem which said that there was a land of wonders in the lee of Morven. This was the countryside around the hill...the 'road by bonnie Bellastraid' and through the Blelack woods to Loch Davan and 'hill-bright Tillypronie'. The hill itself has a harsher beauty, showing at times the cold face of Byron's 'Morven of Snow'. Yet a surprising number of people lived on its inhospitable slopes. From the back region of Easter Morven a Kirk Road served 'a good many inhabitants' making their way to Tullich Church by the Burn of Tullich, or over the shoulder of Creagan Riach to the Pass of Ballater and Monaltrie.

Western Morven was even more heavily populated. In his wanderings over *Mor bheinn,* the big hill, Byron would have seen these remote communities. From them children walked long distances to school in Glen Gairn. In April, 1899, the school log noted that the weather was bitterly cold and that 'even the little ones who have about five miles to come have been here three days of the week'. In 1850 there were seventeen houses in Wester

Morven. Some of these youngsters came from crofts near Morven Lodge. The Ordnance Survey map of 1869 shows four of them — three in ruins, but others have vanished.

Amy Stewart Fraser, in her book in *In Memory Long,* told how her father, the Rev James Lowe, who was parish minister, knew all the *larachs* by studying the Ordnance Survey map of 1869. He often crossed the Hill of Lary from Mullach to Bothanyettie to visit George Coutts, a shepherd who lived there with his wife and family. 'There were numerous larachs nearby', she wrote, 'fast disappearing under juniper and heather where there had been a thriving community, a clachan'.

Bothanyettie, Loin Mhor and Loin Bheag, Bogmuick (*Bog na Muice*), the bog of the pig, Glachantoul (*Glac an t-Sabhail*), Burnside…these were some of the crofts lying in the lap of Morven. Adam Watson and Betty Allan gave Bothanyettie as Bothan Eitidh, meaning a stormy bothy, Surveys carried out by the Grampian archaeological team (now under Aberdeenshire Council) show the remains of deserted settlements at Morven Lodge and by the Morven Burn and its tributary the Allt Salach. Among the ruins of one I saw a rowan tree, planted to ward off evil.

There was said to be an old track going up from Bothanyettie through the Little Slack, but it is difficult to trace now. It probably followed the Allt Coire nan Imireachan, a tributary of Morven burn. The name is said to mean 'burn of the corrie of the flittings, either the movements of shieling to shieling, or the dairy utensils and other effects moved about during summer pasturing on Morven'. The area at the foot of Tom Liath, where the Imireachan burn comes down from Coire nan Imireachan is good shieling country, which seems to back up the 'flitting' theory, but Adam Watson thought it 'fanciful'.

Eight names of former habitations around Morven Lodge were listed in Watson's *Place Names of Upper Deeside.* One was Reid Jimmie's house, which stood by the Morven Burn. Now a ruin, it is still marked (though not named) on the 1:25,000 OS map. Lewie of the Laggan told of a ghostly experience he had when passing the Cairn of the Bokie near the house. 'Just as I got within half a mile o' Reid Jimmie's hoose I grew some frighted gaein' by that carn', he said. 'My hair got stannin' up on my heid like a' that.' When he was past the Carn it 'got a' richt' again'.

Lewie put his fear down to the fact that the cairn was 'where the deid bodies was gotten'. The 'deid bodies' were the bodies of a woman and her daughter lost near the Glack of Morven. But as Lewie said, such stories 'wear oot o' mind', fade away. The green bowl of Morven has been emptied of its myths and legends — and its people. Morven Lodge, bustling with life when the gentry gathered there during the shooting season at the end of last century, met the same fate as the shiels and crofts when it was demolished in 1891. Only traces of the lodge can be seen, but there are still a number of abandoned buildings scattered about the grassy hollow where it stood...the stables, a laundry, the keeper's house and the shepherd's house.

I left Morven to its memories and went south to Lary. I was sniffing the air for the smell of usqueba. This was Gillander country, or had been; they farmed Lary from 1809 to 1949. By all accounts they liked their whisky. I wondered if it was a Gillander from Glen Gairn who featured in an old Gaelic song in which a wife, scolding her husband for his drinking, said bitterly: 'The hole beneath your nose would keep your pocket without a penny.'

At anyrate, the Lary Gillanders seemed to like their whisky better when it was made with the smell of peat reek in their noses —in an illicit still. Gillanders' Still was said to be hidden in the Lary burn near the farm, but according to a Gaelic poem called 'Gillanders' Quaich' it left a lot to be desired:

> I've often drunk strong whisky
> in a bothy on the hill,
> But nothing half so terrible
> As Gillanders can distil.

There are no Gillanders at Lary now. The farm is perched loftily at the end of a road climbing up the Prony from the Fit o' Gairn. It stands in splendid isolation at the top of the Lary brae, with its back to the farm and the track above it curving round Lary Hill to Morven. Harry Anderson, the Lary farmer, has history on his doorstep, for all about him are the ruins of a settlement that flourished three centuries ago, then finally died. The 1696 Poll Book shows nine tenants (eight with wives) living at 'Larie'. Two had sons and there was also a 'cotter (no trade)' who had a wife.

I was told that there had been eighteen families in the vanished township, which suggests that there had been a big increase in population after the 1696 Poll. Certainly, the number of ruins pointed to a larger settlement. There were ruined buildings on the edge of the road to Morven Lodge and all the way down the brae from the farm to Laggan. Laggan Cottage stands beside the Glenfenzie Burn. It was there that my wife, Sheila, spent her summer holidays with the Norrie family in pre-war years. Willie Norrie was a roadman. He and his wife Mary had seven of a family, four girls and three boys. On Saturdays the girls would cycle to the Post Office at the Fit o' Gairn to spend their Saturday pennies on sweeties. In those days, Robert Shaw, the Highland heavyweight, lived at Inverenzie. He had an appreciative audience when he practised putting the shot and tossing the caber on a haugh by the Glenfenzie Burn.

I never discovered where Lewis of the Laggan's 'black thackit hoosie' had been, but between the cottage and the burn there was once a cairn in memory of him. My wife remembers seeing the name 'Lewis' cut in one of the stones. Sadly, the cairn had collapsed into a jumble of stones. There was also a mill at the Laggan at one time. An old picture taken in 1868 shows it as a stone building with a slated roof. It may be that all that remains of it is a ruined wall and gable-end near the cottage, where a handful of wooden sheds have been built.

The old picture also shows a number of farm buildings with thatched roofs, while nearer the mill is a crude, roughly-built 'thackit hoosie' made of stone, wood and sods.. Outside this but-and-ben a woman with a white mutch on her head can be seen working at her spinning wheel. The miller may have been Miller Fraser, who built a 'small hut' near the Laggan Burn for his mother and sister. When his mother died he let old Meg McGregor move into it. Meg is said to have spent her time spinning and carding, so it is more than likely that she was the woman in the picture.

Margaret McGregor, who was born at Tullochmacarrick, west of Gairnshiel Bridge, was the holiest woman in Glen Gairn. Well educated, an avid reader, she went to Mass regularly and prayed at intervals while doing her work. She made shoes for herself from rough wool, with soles cut from old cloth and sewn together with strong twine. She died in 1859 at the age of eighty-two and was buried in the old kirkyard at Dalfad.

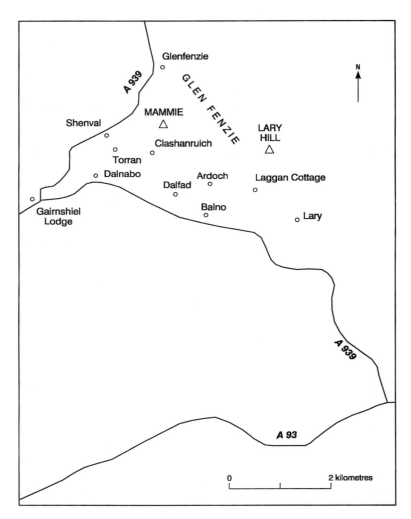

*Map 6. The fermtouns of Gairnside. The clachan at Ardoch was known as the 'Metropoleon' of Gairnside.*

# CHAPTER 6

# THE METROPOLEON

They called it 'the Metropoleon o' the Waterside'. What they meant was that it was Glen Gairn's metropolis; where they said, 'fowk had a'thing amang themselves'. This was Ardoch, one of the biggest clachans on Gairnside, whose fourteen fire-houses* lay on the lower slopes of Mammie Hill, looking down to where the River Gairn sweeps towards the Dee. To the east was Glen Fenzie, while away to the west was the old Brig o' Gairn and the military road over the Glas-choille to Corgarff.

There were a number of approaches to Ardoch. From Laggan in the east a track wound its way along the riverbank, passing Inverenzie and Balno, to where Amy Stewart Fraser's father, the Rev James Lowe, had his manse. It was at Balno that John Reid, the poet of Glen Gairn, was born. He called young Amy the Maid of Gairn and encouraged her to persevere with her writing. He could never have foreseen that she would one day write a series of books on Glen Gairn that would put it on the map.

Today, virtually nothing remains of the manse. Its lawn is a wilderness, the old croquet green buried under a turmoil of shrubs and weeds. The glen that Amy Stewart Fraser knew as a child has gone. From the Fit o' Gairn to Loch Builg, in the shadow of Ben A'an, the land groans under a desolation of abandoned farms and ruined cottages. Glen Gairn, perhaps more than anywhere else on Deeside, has become the 'land of the lost' — and up on Mammie Hill the clachan whose 'fowk had a'thing' now has nothing.

John Reid, who left the glen to join the police in Aberdeen and Leith and later to become a detective with the North British Railway in Glasgow, returned home to find the old mill at the Laggan dismantled, the sluices broken, the miller's workshop in ruins, his house in 'a gloom of silence'.

I approached Ardoch from the west, from the Glas-choille road, down a rough, rutted track that runs under the shoulder of Mammie Hill and passes the House of Clashinruich, built in 1915. It is an imposing mansion, with twenty rooms, but it seems to sit uneasily

* houses with chimneys

*Ardoch 1.*

in its Gairnside setting, surrounded by wild heather and juniper bushes. The ruins of the old Clashinruich chapel can be seen beyond the house. It was built in 1785 by Father Lachlan McIntosh, a priest who tended the Catholic community in Glengairn for sixty-four years, dying in 1846 at the age of ninety-three. He was known as the Apostle of Glengairn.

There was a clachan at Clashinruich in Father McIntosh's time. In her book, *Roses in December,* Amy Stewart Fraser mentioned the last remaining house there. Maggie Maclean's thatched cottage. All that can be seen now is a scattering of stones. Other ruins can be seen on the way from Clashinruich to Ardoch.

The glen is peppered with *larachs.* There is not much left of the grand Metropoleon of the Waterside. Even in its heyday it was said to be 'a nasty guttery (muddy) place' and it was still that when I was there. The only buildings with roofs on them were the farm-house and out-buildings, sitting in a sea of mud and water, with a pair of scraggy gean trees at the front door. The year 1972 had been painted on the door, but what, if anything, it signified I never discovered. Below the farm-house, with its empty windows gaping down to the waterside, ruins and founds of the clachan formed grey patterns of stone on the sodden grass.

I climbed away from it, heading up Mammie, looking for Clachnaschoul (Clach nan Sealladh), the stone of the views. The Rev

Thomas Meany, a Roman Catholic priest who served there from 1888 to 1899, listened to the tales of his Gairnside congregation and jotted them down in two ruled exercise books. From Clach nan Sealladh one of his women parishioners pointed out the houses and the folk in them...the priest's place, for instance, was 'farrest doon', and then there was James Michie's house, which 'wasna sae auld as a puckle o' them', and 'awa' ower the stripe' (stream) was the merchant's shop run by Charlie Caddell, who was 'the first in this watterside to carry rags to the sooth'.

Charlie (his real name was Calder) was Ardoch's entrepreneur — 'well, he med siller oot on't', they said. He drove merchandise between Blairgowrie and Ardoch and over his shop door he had a sign saying 'licensed to retail tobacco and snuff'. Some of his customers were puzzled by it; they thought it said he was licensed to *rattle* tobacco and snuff'.

Father Meany's manuscript, written in broad Doric, told how life had been in the glen long before he became its priest. It dealt with the first half of the 19th century; 'thae times' was how they spoke of it. The priest's house was 'a braw hoose' in those days. Weaver Cattanach had a place ower the dyke and Jean Keir's house was up beside Lachy's stable at the head of the yard. An auld wife called Annie Gow lived in 'a wee bit hoosie' near the 'yaird'. The yard was the heart of the community. It was 'fair oot in the middle o' the village and a'body had a bittie o't for kail and sic like; they couldna hae muckle mair when there wez sae mony o' them'.

Wullie Ritchie, another weaver, had a house at the head of the yard. In one end of the 'hoosachie' he kept his loom; in the other end he kept a coo. Other folk who had 'a'thing among themselves' were Braid Lizzie, who 'didna belong a'thegither to Ardoch'...Lachy with the long white hair...a 'wumman Grant', who lived with her son, Wullie Brown...the shoemaker...Mary o' the Mulloch...Muckle Donald o'Tominturn, who gave the gaugers a run for their money, and Meg Riach, a 'terrible woman and a great smuggler'. Their houses straggled backwards and forwards as if they had 'fa'en oot o' the air'. The burn came down through them and each house had a spout in the water and a 'stroup' (a pump) built up with stones.

From where I stood on Mammie hill, with the remains of the old clachan spread out below me, I could imagine the Ardoch folk wandering up the brae to sit at the Clach nan Sealladh, the stone of the views, losing themselves in the vast canvas of sky and hills that lay before them…Geallaig, the 'white hill' across the water, where King Edward VII had ridden up on his pony with his Inverness cape wrapped about him, distant Mount Keen, white with snow when I was there, and the crofts along the Gairn, their reekin' lums throwing up thin pillars of smoke along the glen.

I tried to pinpoint the places in Father Meany's exercise book, to put life back into the old ruins. One shattered building looked as if it might have been the priest's 'braw hoose', for a dyke in front of it suggested the 'yeirdie' that had been 'richt oot afore it'. I could see the stripe or stream, which seemed to spring from a well, dribbling its way down to the Gairn through a boggy mass of reeds and weeds. It was on the other side of that stream that Charlie Cadell, Ardoch's entrepreneur, had his shop.

But this exercise in nostalgia was pointless, for the view I was seeing was a world apart from the one Father Meany had seen. Lachy and Mary and Lizzie had gone, and all the rest with them; now there was only emptiness. I could almost hear those 'voices on the braes', telling how it had been in those far-off days, a different place, full of life and laughter. 'Sal, it was a hairty ples!' said the woman on Clachnaschoul. They were given to expressions like that — 'Certes! they hinna a hairst amang them!' or, in a bad winter, 'Ma bendezous, meat was ill to get'. More than anything, it was their metropolis, a place where they were 'proheebited fae naething — neither fishin' nor foolin'.'

The land behind me was said to be 'strict', meaning steep and narrow, but Mammie or Maamie is a gentle hill. The name comes from *Mam*, a term given to hills that are soft and round. At anyrate, 'thacket hoosies' clung to its lower slopes as if hiding away from the domination of nearby Morven, *mor bheinn*, the big hill. High on Mammie hill was where Mary o' the Mullach had lived, An Aberdeen archaeological survey located a deserted settlement at Mullach, and its stones lie on top of the hill as if they had been dropped from the heavens. In one marshy corner an old sink lay on its side, while a pipe beside it spat out a steady flow of water.

I left Ardoch and made my way back to the Glas-choille, passing crofts that had once provided a livelihood for many Glengairn families. Now they had all gone, Torran, for instance, was for years the home of the Ritchies. The 1891 Census listed eight Ritchies at the Torran — William Ritchie and his wife Euphemia, their two sons, William and James, and four daughters, The old farm has changed little. The house looks down on the Torran Burn, which on a wild day of high winds in January, 1902, became the scene of unexpected tragedy. It struck the Ritchie family when the Torran burn, which was normally a minor stream, went into spate. May Ritchie, returning from Kirkstyle near the church at Gairnshiel, where she had been collecting a pair of shoes, slipped on a plank spanning the burn and was swept over a waterfall into the Gairn. Her body was recovered from the river more than three weeks later.

Amy Stewart Fraser knew Euphemia Ritchie in later years — to her she was 'Old Mrs Ritchie', wearing a mutch and a black knitted capelet. She remembered, too, her husband, William Ritchie, 'a canny old man', who smoked a black pipe with a silver lid on the bowl, and Willie Ritchie, May's brother. She recalled Willie sowing oats by hand, with a canvas creel slung round his neck and shoulders, swinging his arms in and out until the whole field was covered. There were still Ritchies at the Torran in the years before the last war, when my wife spent her holidays at the Laggan with the Norries.

Tomnavey, Richarkarie and Delnabo were other farms, or former farms, on the way west to Gairnshiel. George Mackie and his wife Norma took over the sheep farm at Delnabo twenty-five years ago. When I last saw George seven years ago he told me how Amy Stewart Fraser had wanted to see the Queen Mother's shiel at Auchtavan in Glen Fearder before she died, so they took her on a nostalgic journey up the Gairn. Writing about it in *Roses in December,* she mentioned seeing scattered larachs in Glen Fearder where there had once been 'a tiny oasis of cultivation and an active community'. It was an excursion into the 'lovely lonely places' that Glengairn's Grand Old Lady said would stay in her memory as long as she lived.

Before taking the same road, chasing the Gairn to Loch Builg, I climbed the steep brae from Gairnshiel to Shenval to take a last look back over Gairnside. 'Shenval' comes from *An Sean-bhaile,* the auld toon. The farmhouse was slowly disintegrating, its roof broken, a huge crack running down the wall at the gable-end. Inside, it was a shell, no door, no windows, the skeleton of a stairway climbing up to nowhere. Shenval sat on the edge of the road, looking as if at any moment it might topple into the glen below. Another coachload of tourists rattling up the brae, you thought, and away it would go.

John Fleming, who was the last of the Flemings in the glen, worked the Shenval croft, ploughing the hard stony ground with a horse and a stot. But other farmers had tilled the Shenval soil long before that. An archaeological survey showed that there had been a township in this corner of Glen Gairn at one time,

'The remains of a depopulated settlement', said the report, 'comprising at least five longhouses and an enclosure, survive on a south-facing slope'. The last time 1 saw the old farm-town it was going the same way; it looked as if one day it would be just another archaeological curiosity, a reminder of what life was like on Gairnside in another age.

The hills reach out to travellers going west. Beyond Gairnshiel the land is bare, often inhospitable, with no sign of a friendly 'reekin' lum'. Yet the *larachs* scattered throughout the glen from Gairnshiel to Loch Builg show that people did live there. It was, in fact, a busy, lively glen, a route taken by drovers going south, and a place where the Glengairn minister had his manse.

Not far from the old hump-backed bridge a wooden bridge crosses the Gairn to the farm of Tullochmacarrick, now deserted, and from it a path runs east to Gairnshiel, passing an isolated building overlooking the river. It is a ruin now, but it was once the manse of Glen Gairn. It was to this remote corner of the glen that the Rev Robert Neil brought his bride in 1847.

In 1943, Robert Neil's daughter, Catherine, wrote a small book about the glen that she loved. Its title was *Glengairn Calling,* and in it she described how 'one house after another' had been pulled down in the glen, pointing out that old inhabitants re-visiting it would 'find many a ruin or *larach'*. Yet she had a vision. When the horrors of war were over, she thought, people might be glad to find a resting-place in this peaceful spot. In her heart she knew it might never happen. 'Perhaps' she said, 'this is only wishful thinking'.

Catherine Neil saw it in its good years, thickly populated, full of 'hardy, friendly, contented people', with old men who had brewed the barley bree slipping up the hills by Glen Doll with their ponies laden with kegs of whisky. The farms were small, mostly hill pasture for black-faced sheep, with enough ground cultivated to supply food for the people and their cattle.

Downhill and across the river were the ruins of the hamlet of Loinahaun. There were six to eight cottages in this clachan when Robert Neil took up his new post. The first thatched cottage was occupied by a weaver and his wife. The weaver was at his loom during the winter, but he had other work to fall back on at other times, acting as a ghillie during the shooting season and taking charge of the bearers when a coffin had to be carried.

Next to the weaver was a tailor, while nearby was Eppie Ogg, who was the 'postie' for Loinahaun, carrying letters to Ballater and returning with incoming mail. Eppie couldn't read, but her neighbour who was dumb, spoke on her fingers and told her where to deliver the letters she had brought back. Not far away is Braenaloin, where another woman 'postie', Jean Gillanders, lived at a much later date. I remember sitting in her house at Ballater while she told me how she had once carried mail into the glens — on horseback.

The ruins of the house of Auchentoul are a little beyond Loinahaun. It is said that seventeen Peter Flemings succeeded each other at Auchentoul. The last Fleming fought at Culloden and was wounded and left for dead. He was wearing a good pair of boots, which were taken off his 'corpse' by an English soldier. Fleming lay in agony while they were removed, showing no sign of life, and he was eventually able to make his way to a nearby house, where he was cared for until he could make his way home to Glen Gairn.

Behind Tullochmacarrick a path climbs round the west face of Fox Cairn to a hill called The Ca'. Time has almost obliterated the Ca' Road, which was an old way from Upper Donside to Glengairn. The old Scots word 'Ca' meant a way for cattle. Farther west, another old drove road, the Camus, went over the hills to Cock Bridge from Easter Sleach, a crumbling ruin on the slopes of Tom Odhar. The farm was reached by a ford across the Gairn.

From these old hill paths you could look straight down the glen, following the glinting course of the Gairn, to the sheep farm at Daldownie, which until 1977 was the last building of any consequence in the glen apart from Corndavon Lodge. On my first visit to Daldownie — 'Doll Dounie', Queen Victoria called it — there was only a ruin to remind you of the old days, but a year later there was nothing.

Daldownie has gone, although the trim-footed ewes still graze on the slopes of Easter Sliach. But the great as well as the good have suffered from decline in the glens. Corndavon Lodge, once a shooting box at the base of the Brown Cow Hill, stands roofless on the banks of the Gairn. It had among its tenants Lord Cardigan of Crimean fame, and in more recent years it was used by members of the Royal Family. Now it is a gaunt and ghostly shell on the way to Loch Builg.

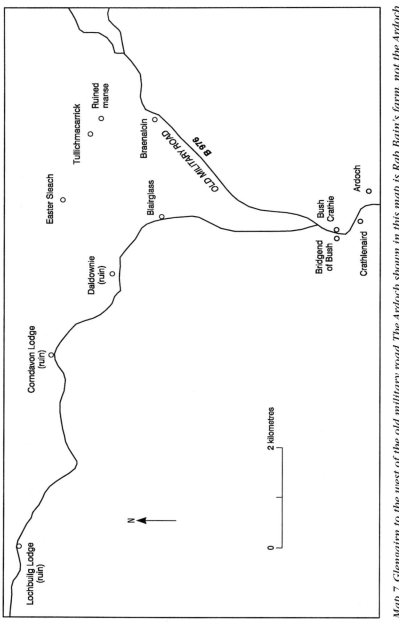

*Map 7. Glengairn to the west of the old military road. The Ardoch shown in this map is Rab Bain's farm, not the Ardoch mentioned in the previous chapter.*

# CHAPTER 7

# 'NOO THERE'S NAEBODY'

**A**rdoch stands at the top of Queen Victoria's Roadie. This is not the 'metropoleon o' the waterside', the Ardoch in Glengairn, but a farm of the same name high above Crathie and Balmoral. The 'roadie' was built for Victoria so that she could rattle up the hill in her horse and gig and look out on Deeside from a viewpoint near the summit of Creag a' Chlamhain. She had a bird's eye view of her domain, with Balmoral Castle below her. But that is in the past. Now, Rab Bain is king of all *he* surveys. He has lived there for over sixty years.

Rab knows the Gairn like the back of his hand. His mother, Mrs Jean Bain, was the last Gaelic speaker on Deeside. Born in London in 1890, she was brought up by relatives in Upper Deeside, first at Knock in Inverey, later at Claybokie. Her aunt and uncle spoke only Gaelic to each other and for a long time 'young Jeanag' couldn't understand a word they said. As she grew up, one of her close friends was Kate Lamont — Ceitidh Chaluim — who was among the last of the inhabitants of Glen Ey before the clearances in 1840.

It was while carrying out research on place names that Adam Watson and Betty Allan heard about the Gaelic-speaking Mrs Bain who lived on a farm above Crathie. On 15 February 1986, Adam and Betty, along with John Duff from Braemar climbed the Queen's Roadie to Ardoch and met Jean's son, Rab. 'Someone told us that he would probably know some local place names', Adam wrote later. It was the beginning of a relationship with Rab and his mother that not only helped in the compilation of the classic work, *The Place Names of Upper Deeside,* but also shed light on a language that was thought to have died out on Deeside in the late 1960s.

Rab, born in Braemar, was only a month old when he and his mother went to live at Daldownie in Glen Gairn. On 6 January 1936, they flitted to Ardoch, a name that means the high point. 'I remember that day', says Rab. 'I min' when we got there we had oor supper aff een o' yon plywood tea boxes lined wi' silver paper. There's a lot o' changes since that time. There wis folk roon aboot us a'wye, noo there's naebody.'

*Rab Bain with his dog.*

Talking about people who had left the glen, he said that most of their houses had been sold or let, 'Fit we ca' white settlers', he added. He didn't seem to resent doctors and businessmen coming into the glen looking for week-end cottages, but he found it hard to understand why it had happened: how it had come about that the whole glen had been emptied of the folk he had known and grown up with.

His mother was the last of the Gaelic speakers and now he says, 'I'm the last o' the Gairnsiders'. He laments the fact that there are no reekin' lums west of Gairnshiel. Tullochmacarrick — 'the Tulloch', he called it — has been left to the wind and rain, and the old manse nearby stands gaunt and ravaged above Loinahaun; Renatton, lying

*Daldownie before it was demolished.*

in a loop of the Gairn, has gone, Easter Sleach stands forgotten up on the brae ('Willie Gordon bade there; he was some boy', said Rab); Daldownie, which Rab went to as a bairn, has been wiped from the map, and away up the glen the ruins of the lodge where Donald MacHardy, a stalker, lived with his wife and family are lost in the heather.

It was to Richarkarie, east of Gairnshiel, that I went to meet Rab. He had leased the grazing on three of the old crofts, Richarkarie, Shenval and Torran, where the Ritchies used to live. In all, he now has 70 acres of arable land and some 2000 acres of hill ground. He has 400 sheep to look after — 'quite enough for an auld pensioner', he said. He likes to tell you that he is getting auld and worn, that his memory has gone, and that his brain isn't as sharp as it once was, but there is a contradictory glint in his eye as he says it and nobody believes him anyway. 'I'm an uneducated person', he said, 'but when I see what education does to some o' them I'm nae sorry. An afa lot o' them hae brains, but they hae nae sense.'

We spoke about folk we knew…Ian Cameron, up at Abergairn ('When you look across tae auld Maggie Fraser's hoose, well, there's ruins on the left-hand side at the Milton Brig. That's far the Camerons originated')…Colin Fraser at Tullochcoy ('I was workin wi' his father the day he was born')…Adam Watson ('I ken Adam fine, he's

*This red-roofed barn is all that is left of Daldownie Farm in Glengairn. Queen Victoria drove past it on her expeditions to the hills and the people on the farm gathered to wave to her.*

gettin' greyer an' greyer')...Donald Grant, whose father once had the Inver Inn...Willie Meston, secretary of the Braemar Royal Highland Society and mine host at the Coillacreich Inn, who had told me I would find Rab at Richarkarie.

I thought of Bill Meston when Rab quoted me an old couplet he knew:

> Tamidhu for boots an' shoes,
> Kyle o' Creich for whisky.

'I think it was aul' Peter Benton, the tailor, that wrote that poem', said Rab. There was another two-liner on the tip of his tongue which was less complimentary to the Inver:

> Piper Hole and Scutter Hole
> Inver Inn for skitter an' din.

The conversation was interrupted by whistles and cries of 'Here, come oot o' that!' and 'Sit doon, ye menace!' Nap, his dog, was friendly and frisky, but Rab said it was a well-bred dog. 'I need a good dog, because I hinna muckle friends mysel'.' He was putting himself down again. Moss, the other dog, had Alsation in him, but was lying quietly watching the sheep.

When I first met Rab six or seven years ago he had another dog. I remember Rab saying with a toothless grin, 'I've got twa teeth an' my dog has ae e'e'. I wondered what had happened to it. 'He was a topper o' a dog that', said Rab. 'He was only eight years' aul' when he died; he had cancer. I used to put him on the road in Crathie wi' up to forty ewes and lambs an' I'd come ower here and the dog would herd them ower to Richarkarie on its own. The aul' Queen Mother has a picture o' him by her car at the top o' the hill road. There was nobody wi' him at a'. He put the sheep aff the road and when they had gone he was roon aboot an' on to the road an' away again.'

Richarkarie was the haunt of John Begg, the one-time whisky smuggler who became 'legitimate' and built the Lochnagar Distillery in 1845. Rab said that Begg had an illicit still in the glen, not far from where we were standing, and when he became 'legitimate' he set up his first still in the barn at Richarkarie, moving to Easter Balmoral after the original distillery there was destroyed by fire.

I left Richarkarie and went over the Glas-choille to Ardoch, searching for old settlements that were on both sides of the road from Crathie to Corgarff. There was a surprising number of ruins just off the Queen's Roadie, lying on what appeared to be the old hill track up to Ardoch, climbing the brae from near Crathie Church. Records in 1814 show only two tenants in Ardoch, which suggests that by that time it was on the decline.

A large number of cockerels and hens were crowing and pecking about the place as I neared Rab's house. In bygone days, Rab would have had to hand one over as rental for his house. In 1814 the rent was a reek hen — a hen paid in lieu of rental. Opposite the house, on the other side of the track, heavy stones, rubble and rubbish were piled under a tree. This, I discovered, was all that was left of the original Ardoch farmhouse. It had been a thatched cottage with an earthen floor and a hole in the roof to let out the smoke from the fire.

It didn't look much, but like so many buildings of its time it crammed more people into it than seemed possible — seventeen was the figure Rab had been told; the tenant and his family, a woman servant, horseman, a young loon, and a domestic servant. It had been a better type of house than many of them, he said. Folk then had ten or twelve of a family.

The present house, built in 1859, sits on a hillock overlooking Balmoral, with the river threading its way down from the Deeside hills. For all its grand view, Ardoch seems to be 'out of the world', an

*The view from above Rab Bain's farm at Ardoch, looking down on Balmoral Castle and the River Dee.*

old farm town that belongs to the past, and Rab says there hasn't been a board touched since they moved into it. It is an isolated spot despite the rush of traffic at the foot of the brae. I couldn't help thinking that it must be a lonely place to live in, particularly for a long-standing bachelor like Rab. Why had he never married? Rab always has an answer to questions like that. 'I'm lookin' for a rich widow wi' a bad cough', he said. 'Wi' *my* luck I'm likely jist to get the bad cough!'

His luck ran out four years ago when he had a brain haemorrhage. He managed to get to his doctor and woke up in hospital in Aberdeen. 'The oil had run oot o' my brain', he says. Much of what happened then is a blank, but he still remembers the consultant — 'a little foreign mannie' — coming to his bedside. He looked at Rab and said, 'We've given your brain a scan and there's nothing there'.

'My God!' said Rab. 'I've had it for sixty-three years, there must be *something* there.'

Five or six hundred yards along the track from Ardoch, opposite the former farm of Lawsie, now with a modern house on the site, was what archeologist Ian Shepherd described in his report as a depopulated settlement. This ruined township was startling in its size, looking as if it had built with outsize stones to withstand the bitter winds that come whistling down the glen. I couldn't help wondering how the drystane dykers of those days had been able to handle such monstrous boulders. 'Wall footings survive to a height of 1m', said the report.

The archeological survey mentioned nine longhouses, two enclosures and a limekiln situated at a height of 370m, on a west-facing slope. The limekiln was easily spotted — it was full to its stony brim with rusted tins, although what they had contained I never discovered. Across at the farm of Lawsie the surveyors had taken note of the footings of two other longhouses.

There was a longhouse at the Knock of Lawsie, a little to the north, and three other longhouses on the east bank of the Rintarsin Burn. Still farther on was the former farm of Rintarsin, where, Rab had told me, there had been a township with 'about thirty reekin' lums'. There was also an old kirkyard there, he said, but it was difficult to find. Rab also told me about another large settlement on the west side of the Crathie-Corgarff road, near Bush. I had heard the name before — Crathienaird, which old people once pronounced Crichie-naird. 'It wis an afa size o' a place', said Rab. 'It was a laird's place…a fair place. There's a lot o' ruins there.'

The laird was Farquharson of Invercauld, who had a holding on his Crathienaird property called Bridgend of Bush, leased to a schoolmaster-turned-farmer by the name of James Brown. Brown married Margaret Leys, the daughter of an Aberarder blacksmith, and it was at Bridgend on December 8 1826, that Queen Victoria's famous servant, John Brown, was born, the second of eleven children. When he was five the family moved to Bush Farm, on the opposite side of the road. No one could have foreseen that in the years ahead Johnny Brown, as Victoria called him, would lead the Queen on her pony past his birthplace on their way home from an expedition to Inchrory. 'Brown led mine on at an amazing pace up the Glaschoil Hill', the Queen wrote in her *Journal*.

The Browns were said to be well-off in comparison with the average crofter in Crathie parish. It was in turbulent streams like the Rintarsin and Crathie Burns and in the moors around them that John Brown learned to fish and shoot. He helped with the farm chores, learning to 'fog the walls', stuffing bits of moss into the nooks and crannies of the farmhouse to keep out the wind. He attended the local school, where Gaelic was the dominant language, but much of his education came from his father.

*The barn at Crathienaird, which is a listed building. John Brown was born near here at Bridgend of Bush.*

The Crathienaird settlement, which must have been an exciting playground for the boy Brown, was described in 1982 as 'the remains of a small township, consisting of five longhouses'. Some houses were subdivided, with varying dimensions. A low bank ran below the enclosure of the present steading and there were two enclosures and depleted field dykes to the north of the settlement.

'Ye'll notice a little tin-roofed aul' barn at Crathienaird', Rab had told me. 'It's a listed building. It was the aul' Crathienaird ferm hoose. It wid a' been the best hoose there, aye. It wid a ha'ed an earth fleer — it still has.' I found the rusty red-roofed barn behind the steading at Crathienaird. It had an earthen floor, as Rab had said, and despite the fact that the thatched roof had given way to a tin roof it still retained a fleeting sense of what life must have been like in the old clachan days.

Two other intriguingly named settlements in that area were linked with Lawsie and Crathienaird in an old verse — Piper Hole and Scutter Hole. When I mentioned them to Rab Bain he recited it for me:

> Piper Hole, Scutter Hole, Crichienaird
> and Lawsie,
> Doon below the Muckle Craig ye'll see the
> kirk o Crathie

Piper Hole was named after a family of pipers called Coutts.They were probably tinkers, for they lived in crude thackit clay biggies and earned a living by working on farms like Crathienaird and the Bush. At harvest time, some went over the Capel Mounth to help with the hairst in the south.

In an area littered with the ruins of old settlements, there have been conflicting reports on the exact location of Piperhole and Scutterhole. When I went up the Piperhole Brae to the Bush the only information I had was that the Piper lay on the north side of the Crathie Burn and the Scutter on the south side. Rab's description pointed the way — the rest I pieced together bit by bit.

Up beside the entrance to Bush Farm a small bridge spanning the Crathie Burn is known as the Piper Brig, while a stretch of the burn running under it is called the Piper Burn. On the south side of the burn, opposite the entrance to the farm, is a large cottage with a conservatory built on front of it.This was originally the farmhouse of Bridgend of Bush, where John Brown was born; now it is a house called Heath Cottage.

On the north side of the bridge an old abandoned cottage with a gaping hole where its door had been stands at the roadside. Ronald Finnie, who has farmed Bush for the past eighteen years, told me there had been a row of five cottages there. The foundations of some of them could be seen on both sides of the last remaining house. This had been a small township — a 'Street' like the line of houses over the Glaschoille at Loinahaun in Glen Gairn. Other ruins could be seen in the woods farther back from the road. The directions I had been given, the name of the brig, the clachan's position north of the burn...everything pointed to this being Piperhole.

On top of all that was the fact that in her book, *In Memory Long*, Amy Stewart Fraser wrote about how she remembered 'a clachan of thatched cottages' at Piperhole on the Crathie side of the Stranyarroch. Her mother had a maid called Lizzie Lamond from Piperhole.The residents there were said to be a 'hardy, independent people, living largely a communal life and working hard for subsistence'.

Queen Victoria often visited the people who lived in the 'thackit hoosies' at Piperhole. She gave them gifts of tea and tobacco, as well as clothing.They were probably 'travelling people' who had settled at Piperhole and Scutterhole. I was told by old Willie Downie of the Lebhal that up the Piperhole Brae the place was 'fu' o' tinkers' at

*Piperhole — the last of a group of cottages at Bush.*

one time. When I asked Rab Bain about it he told me an interesting
tale about the land between the Crathie Burn and the Bush. 'There's
a thing that a lot o' folk dinna ken', he said. 'The bit o' ground atween
the road an' the burn, fae the Bush doon tae the Deeside road, was
Crown land. It's a useless strip. Onybody can graze it, onybody can
shoot it. Aul' Queen Victoria presented that bit o' land tae the
travellin' folk o' Scotland and they own it tee this day.' Rab said that
the occasional tinker — the 'odd een' — still came, adding, 'They're
afa oot o' date that fowk now. They're a' in cooncil hooses!'

Before I left Bush I went in search of Rintarsin. Rab had told me
there were twenty to thirty houses in the township, or, at anyrate,
the ruins of them. I tried to reach it from the Ardoch road, running
through the woods beyond the Lawsie settlement, but without
success. Ron Finnie told me how to get to it by another route.

It took me through a wood bordering the Bush road and on to a
track that climbed up the hill above the Rintarsin Burn. The
foundations of the Rintarsin settlement were scattered across the
hill. Higher up, ruined walls and dykes could be seen among clumps
of juniper bushes and trees. Over the brow of the hill a gate led
into open pasture land, running downhill, stretching away to the
River Dee.

*Corndavon Lodge*

From there I looked down on Lawsie and the ruined township nearby and beyond them to Rab Bain's cluttered farmyard at Ardoch. I could see Balmoral Castle in the distance. The hills formed a spectacular backdrop, Lochnagar, above them all, cold and white. Then I heard the ice cracking under my feet as I crossed the hill, and saw the wreaths of snow streaking the bare hill slopes, and I thought of the people who had once faced bitter winters there.

Some were buried on the hill. Rab had spoken about the old kirkyard above the settlement, hidden away and hard to find. 'Keep climbing up', Ron Finnie had told me. It was in a small circle of trees, he said. I scoured the hill but never found it. It was as if Nature had thrown a cloak over Rintarsin's final resting place.

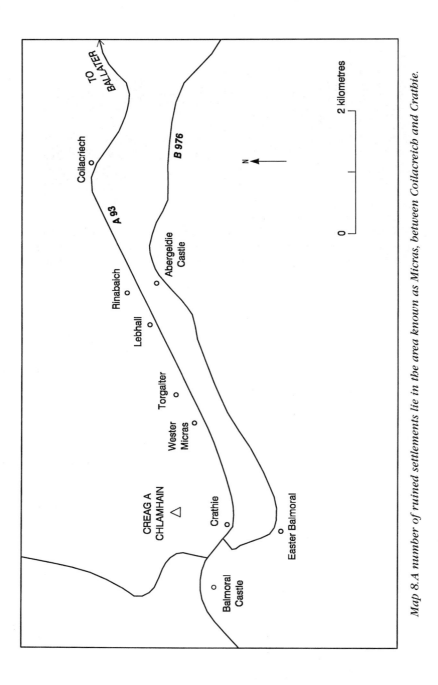

*Map 8. A number of ruined settlements lie in the area known as Micras, between Coilacreich and Crathie.*

# CHAPTER 8
## WILLIE O' THE LEBHAL

When I met Rab Bain, the Ardoch sheep farmer, at Richarkarie in Glen Gairn, he told me he was going down to 'see a lad' at Ballater that day. 'I aye gang doon tee see him on his birthday', said Rab. The lad he was going to visit was Willie Downie, who once farmed at the Lebhal and now lives in Craigard House Residential Home. It was his ninety-eighth birthday.

Willie may have been within striking distance of his century, but according to Rab he was still like a young loon. 'If he sees oot this century', he said, 'he'll hae seen the *whole* o't and he'll hae lived through three centuries. A lot o' folk live to be a hundred, but there's nae mony see a whole century. If he gets intae 2000 he'll be some boy — he'll need twa telegrams fae the Queen!'

Rab was surprised to learn that I had already heard of Willie Downie. Long ago he was a boyfriend of a Ballater lass called Mary McLaren, who married a railway driver, Bill Rae. They were my in-laws and when, in her old age, Mary's mind went back to the folk she knew in Ballater it was almost inevitable that the name of Willie Downie of the Lebhal would drift into the conversation.

Willie is a mine of information about places and people on Deeside; he helped Adam Watson and Betty Allan in their research for *The Place Names of Upper Deeside.* He was born and brought up at the Lebhall, pronounced Level — from *Leth-bailie,* the half-toon — about four miles west of Ballater, and his father and grandfather were there before him. So it was to Willie Downie that I went to find out about that stretch of Deeside from Coilacreich to Crathie, where the remains of old settlements cling to the braes above the Dee.

Fresh-complexioned, smartly dressed, his mind as sharp as a pin, Willie looked well short of the ninety-eight years he had been celebrating. He remembered Mary McLaren as though it had been yesterday — 'aye, a good-lookin' deem', he said — and as for Bill Rae, he 'kent him weel'. He remembered the Norries at the Laggan and Bob Shaw practising putting the shot at Inverenzie, and he spoke about Rab Bain's father, Willie Bain, whom he had known at both

*This ruined farmhouse at the Lebhal was occupied when Willie Downie was a boy.*

Daldownie and the Ardoch. He knew Richarkarie and the Torran, where Rab grazed his sheep, and he remembered the last folk at Shenval, up on the brae, its farmhouse crumbling away as the years went by. He had heard that someone had bought the place, but if that was so they would have to start from scratch and build again,' I kent a' the Glengairn folk', he said.

He also knew Loinmuie, a 'lost' clachan I had been searching for in the hills above Birkhall (see Chapter 10). He remembered 'beasts grazing there' and he had known James Stewart at Altcailleach, the farm which took over Loinmuie. Stewart had been a gamekeeper in Glen Muick.

When I spoke about Loinmuie, Willie began to recite parts of a poem he had heard, struggling with half-forgotten words...' Loinmui wi' its auld rodden tree...my friends...cherished memories'. Sadly, the old verse had slipped from his mind, but he said that his mother, Mrs Euphemia, had known 'the whole history of it'. In fact, Mrs Downie could still recite it at the age of 103 years.

The poem had gone 'up and down fae the top o' the Muick to the bottom' and had been written by a man who had gone abroad. 'He climbed some hill before he went away and wrote it', said Willie. It was more than likely that the hill was Loinmuie itself and that the poem was a farewell to a place he might never see again. Later, I discovered that it had appeared in Adam Watson and Betty Allan's place-name book. The verse Willie was trying to recite went:

Frae the braes o Tom nam Buachaillean*
An the rigs o Aultonrea,
Frae the...o...Loinn Muighe,
Wi' its auld rodden tree.

Willie spoke about how he started work as a loon with his father at the Lebhal, and how he 'biggit stacks' and helped with the ploughing. 'It was a gey hard existence', he said. The old farmhouse was at the back of the present house and he remembered folk staying in it. In the old days, he said, there had been four farms taken into the Lebhal. 'They called them farms, but they weren't big farms, although they all had a pair of horse.'

When I left Willie I headed for the Micras, going first to Tomidhu, which I had seen from Creag Chlamhain, above Rab Bain's farm. The Tomidhu farmhouse stands where the old Deeside Road left the line of the turnpike and swung north-west on its way to Crathie. Betty Grant was born at Tomidhu and has lived there all her life. When her husband, Willie Grant, died she let the land out to another farmer. Now she sometimes looks after his sheep with her collie dog, Dal.

Tomidhu for boots and shoes...there had never been a souter there, according to Betty, so maybe the lines that Rab Bain had quoted had been about the footwear fashions of some previous tenants — in the same way that another verse had tilted at Inver's 'skitter and din'.

Boots, at anyrate, were needed to tramp the dubby track that came down from West Micras to join the old Deeside Road. This was a 'Kirk Road', one of a number of connecting roads between the townships that lay along the face of the brae from West Micras to Rinabaich. These settlements are still there today, but now they lie in ruins, their crumbling walls forming strange shapes and patterns on the slopes below the Rathad Geal, the White Road. There was a school there where the Deeside historian the Rev John Grant Michie, once taught.

'The Micras' was a general name for all the farms between Tomidhu and Rinabaich, although the area was divided into Easter, Wester and Mid Micras. The name was said to mean 'bog', although

---

*A former farm behind Aulltonrea in Glen Muick.

*Betty Grant outside her house at Tomidhu, near Crathie.*

others thought it meant 'a sunny place'. I went to West Micras from Tomidhu by the new Deeside road not the old one, because I had been told that heavy rain had made it boggy. According to Willie Downie, there had once been 'two, three placies' at Wester Micras. John Grant Michie, who was born in Micras on 1 January 1830, gave a detailed description of the original township in his book, *Deeside Tales,* published in 1872. He was an old man when Willie was a lad.

Michie said there were eleven inhabited houses at West Micras when he was a boy. Three were small farms, with arable land consisting of ten to fourteen acres and hill pasture. There were also three crofts with three to four acres of land and no hill pasture. Each was supposed to keep a cow, but never did, and they lived by begging or bartering for work done to farmers. In addition to the farmers and crofters, there were five cottars 'with no land beyond a kailyard'. As the old race of crofters died out, their holdings were added to the farms.

When I went up the farm track to Wester Micras I could see the ruins of cottars' houses on the hill. Ian Esson, who is the tenant farmer of West Micras, thinks nothing of the *larachs* that lie about his fields; he scarcely notices them, for they are as familiar to him as the sheep-pens and hen-houses scattered about the farm. He spoke about the sheep and the 'puckle hens' that he had, but it was more than a 'puckle', there were hen-hooses everywhere.

Ian is the son of Jock Esson, who was for many years a shepherd at Auchtavan in Aberarder — the last shepherd there before the cottage became a shiel for the Queen Mother. He was at Auchtavan from the 1920s, later moving to Balmore and finally to West Micras. In his early days he thought nothing of walking from Auchtavan to the mart in Aberdeen with 500 lambs. It took him seven days — and the price he got for his sheep was 16/- a head.

Up behind the hill, wandering about the ruins, I wondered what sort of house John Grant Michie had lived in. In *Deeside Tales* he gave a detailed description of the Micras — 'a clachan built of turf or divot, or stone and clay at the best, with nothing but timber lums and pitiful small windows.' He wrote about his own house as a 'poor croft' which provided his family with 'both food and clothing', but it was one of the three small farms mentioned in his book and must have been a good deal superior to the homes of the cottars and their kailyards.

The farmhouses had dung-heaps directly in front of them, sometimes only a few feet from the door, and the cottars' houses each had a pig-stye at the back, probably a hen-house, and always an ash-pit. Old traditions die hard, for when I went to Rinabaich I noticed a pail of ash sitting at the door. The *better* houses were buts and bens, with a bed, or maybe two, in each, and one or two in the passage between them. The cottars' houses had no but, 'except when it was used as an apartment for fowls to roost in'. The hens got the benefit of the heat from the 'ben' end, as well as the smoke, which was why they were always the plumpest and fattest.

The first part of the spring work was called the *ait seed,* oat seed, followed by the *beer seed,* barley, which required a lot of manuring.' When the muck's a' oot the bere seed's done', it used to be said. Potatoes and turnips came next, and then a week at the moss and two or three days making the hay and clipping the sheep. Women did most of the harvest work, but it was the men who built and thatched the stacks. When the harvest was completed the men went gadding about the country — *straiking,* they called it, shooting by day and dancing by night and drinking a good deal of whisky at both.

In Michie's boyhood days the people made their own clothes and provided their own food. 'Even the croft of from three to four acres, nearly all under oats and potatoes, were supposed to supply enough for a family of about the same number of individuals, and the small farms supplied whatever deficiency there was in payment of work rendered. Seldom was money given; anyone offering it was considered to be rich. All the cottars had a drill or two of potatoes on an adjacent farm given in exchange for the manure of the ash pit. A pig was killed at Martinmas and a ham cured for use throughout the year.'

So that was the annual round of the clachan dwellers. I was thinking of it when I left West Micras and crossed the fields to Torgalter, avoiding what Willie Downie had said was 'an afa nasty road' to the farmhouse. In fact, an Aberdeen doctor and his family had moved into the house the previous year and the old track had been repaired and made fit for traffic. But I was glad I had taken the 'high road' across the fields, for it opened up a breathtaking view of Upper Deeside. John Grant Michie thought so; he said that the farmhouse of Torgalter commanded 'one of the finest views of the valley of the Dee to be obtained from any point between Ballater and Balmoral'. His grandfather farmed Torgalter before moving to another small holding.

Directly opposite Torgalter was Craig nam Ban, better known as the Witches' Hill because they burned old and innocent women on its summit, while at its foot, half-hidden in the trees, was Abergeldie Castle, where a maid called Katie Rankine was branded as a witch and taken up the hill to be burned at the stake. Prince Albert's Cairn poked its pyramid head above Creag an Lurachain on the Royal estate at Balmoral and sweeping through the countryside was the River Dee, 'the silver river', as Michie romantically put it, 'threading its way with ceaseless song to its far off home in the deep'. The distant hills were grey and hazy and dominating them all was Lochnagar, its ridge glinting icily in the sun, its corries white with snow — Byron's dark Lochnagar, rising, in Michie's words, 'head and shoulders above the rest'.

There was once a small clachan where the Torgalter Burn empties itself into the Dee, its existence largely dependent on a mill and a boat that operated between Abergeldie Castle and the north side of the river. The boathouse was also an alehouse known as Clinkums. It was in this quiet corner of Deeside that the normally passive Torgalter Burn burst its banks in the flood of August 1846, and roared down on a small cottage on the edge of the water. Inside it was Auld Janet, screaming for help, while a woman looking on cried out for someone to 'save the poor body'. Rescuers tore a hole in the roof and hauled her out before the building was swept away, but Janet had lost her mind and died a few weeks later. I was shown the foundations of what were said to be her 'hoosie', but I was never certain that it was Auld Janet's home.

The farms of Torgalter and neighbouring Greystone were both hamlets of considerable importance at one time. Many years ago I spent a holiday at Greystone, where Willie Downie's daughter lived. It was a hot, hot summer and we lay by the Dee and soaked up at the sun, going back for tea at the farm and making friends with a tame duck called Jockie. The farmhouse at Torgalter has been modernised and extended, so that — apart from the ruins in the surrounding fields — there are few reminders of the old clachan days. There is, however, an interesting link with the past behind one of the farm buildings — a built-up, grass-covered platform with a hole in the middle. This was a circular horse-gang, used for threshing where water power was unavailable. Horse-gangs consisted of raised platforms round which a horse or pair of horses walked, turning by means of a shaft the gearing in the middle, so that power was carried through an underground beam to the mill inside the barn.

I left Torgalter with a mystery unsolved. The name is supposed to come from *Torr a' Ghealtair,* meaning 'the hillock of the timid fellow'. Who was the timid fellow? Why was he so fearful? I never found out. I was on my way to Rinabaich, where I was to find the ruins of an old township that seemed to have defied the years, reluctant to turn to rubble and dust like so many others I had seen. The farmhouse sits in the middle of this settlement, caught up in a time-warp. When you drive up the drive from the Deeside road the shells of clachan buildings loom up on either side of the farm road. There are *larachs* in front of the house, more on the banks of the Easter Micras Burn, which tumbles down the west side of the farm, and more still farther up the hill, where there was once a dam feeding the clachan's mill.

There are substantial remains on every side. It is easy to put roofs and lums on them in your imagination and draw a mental picture of what Rinabaich was like two or three centuries ago. Peggy Fraser, who has lived there since 1967, told me that the previous occupant, Molly Farquharson, whose father and grandfather farmed the land,

*Ruins at Rinabaich.*

estimated that there were twenty-one reekin' lums in the settlement. G M Fraser, in his book, *The Old Deeside Road,* said that 'among the deserted dwellings of Easter Micras one cottage is left out of seventeen fire-houses'. That was in 1921.

The 'one cottage' was obviously Peggy's house. Whatever the number of 'fire-houses', nobody bothers about them now. Peggy said that some people had come out from Aberdeen University to look at the ruins and were interested in the fact that the corners of the walls were all rounded. They left and she never saw them again. The old road, 'now grass-grown and long disused', was noted by G M Fraser. It can still be seen running past Peggy's door, which means that it must have gone through the middle of the old clachan.

From Peggy's window you can see Lochnagar. She has a great love of the hills and still goes walking in them. John Grant Michie felt the same way about the mountains on his doorstep. He climbed Lochnagar several times and crossed all the passes between the Capel and the Cairnwell.

About half a mile west of Rinabaich is the Lebhall, where old Willie Downie lived for so many years. When Willie left the Lebhall it was taken over by George and Duncan Kerr, from Auchallater. He and his brother came from the Corgarff area, not far from Cock Bridge, but Duncan was working in Dundee until a few years ago. He was sawing wood when I met him. I half-expected to see the old abandoned farmhouse nearby, but Duncan said, no, it was up the hill. 'I'll show you where it is', he said, and went stamping off up the brae.

We passed a ruined building, one of the 'placies' that Willie had mentioned. It had a rowan tree beside it, planted to ward off evil spirits. 'I always look for the rowan tree', said Duncan. Turbulent burns poured down the Micras braes, feeding the hungry Dee. The hill was sodden, squelching with water. Up ahead I caught my first glimpse of the old house, one of its gable ends sticking up like a broken tooth. Willie had said it was an 'east and west' house — two houses linked to make one — but it was too far gone to see the division. The name Lebhal means 'half-toon', but whether or not it had anything to do with the 'east and west' arrangement I never discovered. What Willie remembered most was that it had a 'hingin' lum', but all traces of it had long since gone. There had been another hanging lum down below in the wash-house.

'They certainly built high on the hill', I said to Duncan. 'They're higher than this', he replied, and off we went again into a jungle of ferns. There had been too little snow that winter to flatten the ferns, with the result that they made walking difficult, catching our feet and hiding what was under them. Despite our slow progress, however, the secret of the Micras braes slowly came to light, for under these dried-up stems and fronds were the remains of the original settlement at the Lebhall.

Duncan pushed his way through the ferns, pointing first to one ruin, then another, 'founds' laid out in a familiar pattern, marking what had been a fair-sized community. Finally, we left them and made our way downhill. Above one of the burns we found a huge lime kiln on the edge of the water. Wherever you go in the Land of the Lost you find kilns — corn kilns and lime kilns. Corn-drying kilns were usually circular, with a drying floor and a bowl-shaped drying chamber. Some were built into slopes or banks, facing the prevailing wind, while others were built as part of kiln barns, where the winnowing could be done in shelter. Near the Lebhal kiln was what appeared to be the stones of a building like Auntie Janet's 'hoosie'.

The light was dimming as we made our way back to the farm. There was a sudden chill in the air and the clouds were dipping over the distant hills. Old Lochnagar was putting on its nightcap — it was time to go home.

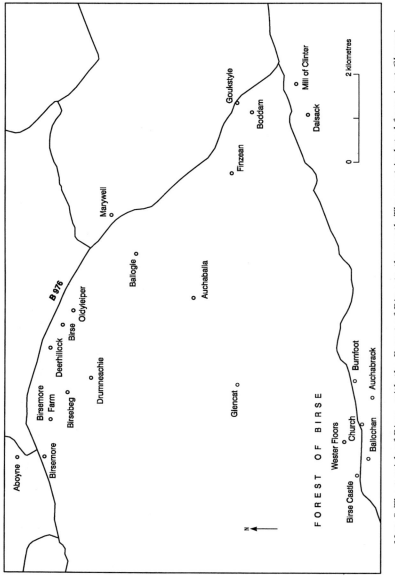

*Map 9. The parish of Birse, with the Forest of Birse to the south. The most isolated farm is at Glencat.*

# CHAPTER 9
# OOT O' THE WORLD

The hills close in on the Forest of Birse like a giant fist. In the shadow of Birse Castle, hill tracks fan out in every direction through Glencat to Ballogie, over the hills by Carnferg to Newmill, up to St Colm's Well and the Firmounth Road, and south from Ballochan to the Fungle and Tarfside.

These were the ancient ways into Birse. I have often walked them — and they have always reminded me of an old Deeside saying, 'Oot o' the warl' and into Birse'. That must have been said when Birse was more isolated, wilder and more remote, a land where the cateran rode. Today, the world has invaded the parish, It has even been said that it is becoming suburban.

The lands and forest of Birse originally belonged to the Bishops of Aberdeen. When they were granted to them by King Alexander II in 1242 they divided the arable part of it into twenty-four 'touns' or holdings…the fermtouns whose Gaelic names have come down the years to the present day, names like Balnaboth, *bailie nam both,* the town of the bothies: Balfiddie, *bailie na feada,* the town of the whistling wind; Ballochan, *the town of the little marshy place.*

Ten miles long and ten miles broad, the parish has a land area of 31,591 acres. It was divided into three portions. The first ran along the right bank of the River Dee and was known as the Six Towns — Birsemore, Birsebeg, Drumneachie, the Kirkton, Balfour and Kiminity. Glencat and Mid Strath lay in the centre and the third area, Feughside, included Finzean and the Forest of Birse. The parish church was in the Deeside section, which meant that up till the 19th century Feughside folk had a long trek over the hills to get to kirk.

Ballochan, crouching in the lap of the hills below Birse Castle, is 'oot o' the world' more than most places in the parish, except perhaps, Glencat. It was from Ballochan that I made my way to the Six Towns, following the footsteps of those ancient kirkgoers, tramping up the Fungle and past the Gwaves (a steep ravine on the Burn of Auldgairney), going north to Carnferg and down the Birse Burn to Newmill. Robert Dinnie, father of the famous Donald Dinnie, mentioned Newmill in his *Account of the Parish of Birse* in 1865.

It lay, he said, in the elbow of the hills to the south of Drumneachie. A family of Rosses had it from the late 17th century to the middle of the 18th century.

'The old mansion of the Rosses has now disappeared', wrote Dinnie, 'but a good house of two stories graces the spot and is let as shooting quarters by the Marquis of Huntly.' The good house of two stories is still there, but it is now occupied by a gamekeeper and the Newmill land has passed into the hands of Alisdair McConnach at nearby Drumneachie.

Drumneachie lies on a quiet back road that breaks away from the South Deeside Road at Birsemore Loch, where George V's consort, Queen Mary, often had a picnic tea at Lady Cowdray's cottage. It passes the farms of Birsemore and Birsebeg and loops round by Balfour to rejoin the main road near Birse Church. Alisdair McConnach was born at Drumneachie. His father, George McConnach, came to it in the 1930s from Craigindinnie Croft, a wet area near Birsemore Loch which was known as the Bog. Alisdair's brother, Neil, farms Deerhillock.

Back in 1696, there were ten families living on the Drumneachie land as tenants or sub-tenants. They included a 'webster' (weaver), a cottar, two tradesmen, servants and a grassman. A grassman, or, colloquially, a girseman, was a tenant with no land attached. Yet there is virtually nothing left to show that this was once a busy township. Out in Alisdair's yard a rickle of stones beside a covered-over well is thought to be the remains of a house, and other 'founds' can be seen in the surrounding fields. On a hill behind the farm is a ruin at what was known as Babbie's Park. Alisdair's father often spoke about the woman who ran a croft there.

Going east from Birsbeg and Drumneachie you come out on the Aboyne road near the farm of Oldyleiper. From there the road runs south to Marywell, which, with its little shoppie and Post Office, was well-known to hundreds of travellers. Now the Post Office has been shut down and the shop has become Sarah Butterworth's coffee shop and art gallery, displaying paintings by her father, Howard Butterworth, the well-known Glenmuick artist.

So Marywell, no longer the centre of the Birse universe, faces the sort of change that has swept through the whole of Deeside over the years. Back in 1696 there were two tenants at 'Marywall', plus a weaver, a blacksmith, a tradesman, a grassman — and a grasswoman. Grasswoman were familiar in this part of Deeside in the old days.

There was also a chapman called James Aberdeen, who was 'there *in familia* with his mother'. Marywell was accustomed to chapmen; they were there in force on the day of the Marywell Market:

> The chapmen were plenty, some roarin' aloud,
> 'My wares are the best, and nane half so gude.'

Robert Dinnie wrote these lines in a long poem about the Marywell Market and the 'queer fowk an' things' that you saw there…spoons, ladles, caups, cogs, Birse bodies wi' bunnets full of bread, wives with 'frowdies an' ribbons that dazzled yer e'en'. Sandy the souter, Will the weaver, Jock the piper, Willie the miller and Johnnie the blacksmith were all there, 'weetin' their thrapples', but Will had a sad end to his day. He 'pree'd (tasted) Janet's ale' too well and his wife turned up and 'leish't him aff doun the clachan'.

Outside Sarah Butterworth's shop, on top of a brae behind the coffee shop, I could see a roofless building silhouetted against the sky. This was a farmhouse with the tongue-twisting name of Torquhandallochy, or, if you take the 1696 version, Tarquhundlacie. Pronounced Torfunlachie, it comes from *Torr ceann dalach*, meaning 'the hill of the head of the field', which is a fairly accurate description of it. In the year of the Poll Book there were two tenants there.

Bob Thomson, grieve on the Ballogie estate's Home Farm, told me that local folk who couldn't get their tongues round Torquhandallochy simply shortened it to Torams. Its roof, he said, had been taken off after the last war to avoid taxes. We bent over a map and picked out other ruins on the estate, among them Arntilly and Arntillyhard, which were linked by an old drove road. Here, the name Arntilly means 'the little height of the knoll'.

The Burn of Cattie runs past Ballogie House. In 1730, William Robbie of Arntilly, 'sometime residenter in Barbadoes', built a bridge over the burn — the first stone bridge in the parish. In the Muckle Spate of 1829 the water of Cattie broke through the west side of the laird's garden, poured into the kitchen and flooded the house. John Birss, a local poet, wrote about the Cattie's intrusion:

> She went to call upon the laird
> The nearest way without regard,
> Through hotbeds and apple trees,
> And gart the berry bushes hies;

Sic company he wasna seekin',
She put his kitchen fire fae reekin'.

During my wanderings through Feughside I was thinking of another poet who wrote about the Muckle Spate of '29 — David Grant of Affrusk. Grant made his name with his poem, a Doric classic, but John Birss remained in the literary shadows. Nevertheless, I was interested in him because of his name. The surname Birss was common a century or so ago, but now it has gone. The last man in Birss to spell his name the old way was William Birss, tenant of the farm of Slidderybrae in Ballogie. I had gone to Slidderybrae to see him, only to find that he had died some time before. A bachelor, he was the fourth generation of his family to farm Slidderybrae.

When I was in Ballogie, a new tenant was moving into Slidderybrae. It was the end of the Birss era. Only a short distance away, however, I found another link with the Birss's of Birse, for new faces were also to be seen at the Mill of Cattie. Mrs Evelyn Hall and her husband, Frank, were settling into a converted steading at the Mill and had named it The Old Byre. Living in Aboyne, they had moved to Birse because their roots were there. Frank Hall's grandfather was a Birss — Frank Birss.

The Mill of Cattie has put history into reverse. A century ago, the old settlements shrunk into smaller units until finally all that remained was one farm. Here, the opposite has happened. The farmhouse, which stood on its own for so long, was still there, but the byre had become a modern home, the mill was being converted into a house, and a building across from the Old Byre was also being converted. It was to be named the Bothy. So a modern 'clachan' had come to life in Birse.

Across the Burn of Cattie is a farm called the Shannel. Ian Alcock, a stockbroker from Berkshire, came north from London and took over the Shannel twenty-three years ago to work it as an organic farm. A turkey cock was fanning its tail in grand passion, circling its mate, when I arrived. Hens clucked about the yard and a tame deer called Keir watched us from an enclosure. Ian said it could quite easily jump over the fence and escape, but it never bothered. On the other hand, wild deer jumped *into* the pen and Farmer Alcock was waiting to see if a pregnancy was on the way.

Shannel and its neighbour at Tillyteach, which is occupied by Hugh Parson, a helicopter pilot, were originally part of Inverchat, whose mansion house stood in a field near the farm. In Robert Dinnie's time a piece of the mansion and part of a garden wall could still be seen, but all that marks the site now are two ash trees and an oak.There is, however, still one link with the past — a stone lintel, taken from the old house which has been built into the wall of the farm steading. It carries the two sets of initials and a date, with a heart in the middle:

167 R S * M K 76

The date is a bit muddled, but it is supposed to show the year the house was built.The initials are that of Robert Stuart, the Inverchat laird, and Margaret Keith, his wife. They had three sons, George, Robert and Henry, and two daughters, Jane and Margaret.The oldest son, who inherited the estate, had a nickname that spread fear and terror in the neighbourhood — Billiebentie.

Billiebentie was a giant of a man. His vest could have enfolded three ordinary-sized men. It was said that he was riding to Torquhandallochy one day when he coughed so hard that his horse fell to the ground with a broken back. Robert Dinnie told another story about a woman in Slidderybrae who, at her wit's end with a badly behaved boy, asked Billiebentie if he could frighten him just a little so that he would be more pliable. Billiebentie said, yes, he could. He took the boy away, walked with him to the Cattie, and held his head under the water until he drowned, 'Of course', wrote Dinnie, 'the woman got little more trouble with her boy'.

The tales about Billiebentie's deeds, or misdeeds, were probably exaggerated, but he was certainly hated by Birse folk.There was an old saying, still remembered in Dinnie's time, which suggested that they wished him only the worst:

> O a' God's people hae a care,
> But Billiebentie dinna spare.

I left Billiebentie and the Shannel and set off to follow the Burn of Cattie to its source at the head of Glencat.The road runs past Arntilly, which Bob Thomson said was a ruin. It must have been a sizeable place in its time, for in 1696 there were two tenants and their wives there. In total, there were no fewer than twenty-two people making a living from it, and in addition to that a tailor, William Leslie, lived there with his wife.

*The road to Glencat. The tree rises above a ruined house. The track over the hills to the Forest of Birse can be seen in the distance, left.*

Two miles from Marywell, the road breaks clear of the forest. Beyond the beeline a rough track drops down into the glen, where the Cattie burn comes sneaking out of the hills and runs through a green bowl where Glencat farm hides away from the world. Beyond it, another dirt track climbs out of the glen and goes through the hills to Birse Castle and Ballochan. From the edge of the woods to the north, I watched a tractor coming snail-like down the steep hill to the farm. Doug Petrie, the Glencat farmer was driving it. He has land at Ballochan.

The Petries have been in Glencat for nine years. Ann Petrie told me that they had the choice of living at Ballochan, but they plumped for Glencat because it had a better road in winter. Ann comes from the Cairn o' Mounth. 'I went from one hill to another', she said. She accepts her lot without complaint, or not much of it, for being 'oot o' the world' has its compensations. We looked back the way I had come. Ruined cottar houses lay off the track and down by the Cattie Burn. The people who lived in them would have been Anne's neighbours in an earlier age. At the beginning of last century there were twenty 'thackit' houses — and twenty families — in the glen.

Not many people go over the hill to Ballochan by car. Winter had roughed up the track, I was told, so I decided to take the long way round to the Forest of Birse, back the way I had come and down by Boddam and Drumhead to the Feugh. Boddam was probably originally called Bottom or Botham; Bothmamfauld in Skene means 'the bottom of the valley', which equally applies to the Boddam in Birse. At anyrate, the Rev Joseph Smith, minister at Birse for more than forty years, who was a bit of a story-teller, once described what happened at the wedding of a tenant in 'a small possession called Bottom' on the Finzean estate. The ceremony was over and it was time for the bridegroom to kiss the bride, but he seemed too embarrassed to do it publicly. The minister, waiting impatiently, suddenly spoke up with a piece of advice that brought a gasp and a giggle from the guests. 'Kiss her, Bottom', he cried, 'Kiss her!'

The names of farms strung along the Feugh seem to leap out of David Grant's poem on the Muckle Spate...Dalsack, whose dyster escaped 'wi' naething save his harn sark', Clinter, where 'plish-plash the water skelpit in', and Ennochie, whose 'cluckin' hen wis sittin' in a kiss' and was carried down the Burn o' Frusk. There was speculation about what happened to it:

> Gin she were carri't to the sea
> Afore her ark gaed wrang,
> An' maybe spairt by Davie Jones
> To bring her cleckin' oot,
> Gin she wid rear them like a hen
> Or like a water coot.

When you travel along the dipping, winding road to Ballochan, you begin to sense what it must have been like in the Forest of Birse in the days when Mathew, Bishop of Aberdeen, was granted — 'for the welfare of his soul and the souls of his ancestors' — all the lands of Birse. The old names were given in the Bishop's list of 'touns',

*Achabrack — the last house on a settlement at the Forest of Birse.*

among them Duchter Birse, Erbentuly, Parce, Drumenathy and Innercat. There are still signs of earlier communities at 'Parcie' and other places. When I was at Shannel (Invercatt), Ian Allcock told me about land on a hill behind his farm known as Whisky Nellie's garden. There were no ruins, only a spring, so maybe Nellie had being doing a bit of illicit distilling.

The Bishop was given the Forest of Birse in 'free and perpetual Elemosina'. But life was difficult and dangerous for those early settlers. The Forest of Birse provided shelter for cateran who plundered the tenantry of the surrounding countryside. The Grants and Mackintoshes frequently lifted the 'marts' and 'muttons' of Deeside and 'retired to the friendly shelter of the Forest'. Deadly battles took place between the raiders and the raided tenants.

A cattle grid marks the end of the public road. Before reaching it, a boarded-up house can be seen in a field near a tributary of the Feugh. This is Achabrack, the last house in a settlement that had at least half a dozen tenants. Near the house is a small chaumer with a lum and a fireplace, while beyond that is a red-roofed steading. Farther up the stream are the foundations of other buildings and

*The Kirk of the Forty Reekin' Lums at the Forest of Birse.*

nearer the Feugh, where an old stone bridge crosses the burn, a modern bungalow stands on the site of a former croft called Burnfoot. Peter Littlejohn, a gamekeeper on the Ballogie estate, has lived there for ten years.

The last man to live in Achabrack was Henry Duncan. Born there in 1907, he lived out his life in that lonely spot until he died in 1977. Alisdair McConnach knew Henry; he recalled how he used to come over to Aboyne from Auchabrack on horseback to get his supplies. The way he told it made me suspect that it was the horse, not Henry, who found the way back. Coming from such a desolate place, one could hardly blame him.

Half a mile from Auchabrack, beside the cattle grid, a path goes down to the Forest of Birse Church, which served as both a school and a church. It was known as the Kirk of the Forty-seven Reeking Lums, but whether or not the name applied to the whole forest, or only to the Birse-Ballochan area, seems uncertain. There are ruins near the track from the Kirk to Ballochan and Alistair Thomson, the Dunecht estate keeper at Birse, has seen others scattered about the area. Some lie below his house at Wester Floors, where the Burn of Auldgarney runs into the Feugh. He believes that the forty reekin' lums *were* at the top of the glen. He may be right, for at one time there was a school in this corner of Deeside.

Across the hills to the west, beyond the Firmounth road, is Glentanar, which had its share of ancient settlements. Old records going back to the early 17th century refer to 'the Dauch lands of Waternarie and Tullicarne and the Dauch of Bowlane Dalquhing Foulbog and Etnich, the croft of Braelyne and the croft called the Alehouse Croft'.

Some of the old names are still familiar today, among them Dalquhing (Dalwhing), Tullicarne (Tillycairn), Braelyne (Braeloine) and Etnich (Etnach). Others have gone. Bordland, or the Borlan' as it was called, was described as a settlement with 'a very good inn, where the forrester lives'. William M Alexander said it was 'a community, now extinct', but in 1696 there were thirty people living there. The Poll Book for that year shows one tenant, ten sub-tenants, and a cottar in the township, plus five servants, most of them with wives. There was also a shoemaker.

Braelyne or Braeloine was another settlement. The old mansion house of Braeloine stood on the site of St Lesmo Chapel, built by the eccentric laird of Glentanar, Sir William Cunliffe-Brooks. The house was the centrepiece of a busy 17th-century community known as Braeloine and Knockieside. It supported a meal mill, several souters' shops, a merchant's shop, an inn and fifteen houses — and the Alehouse Croft. Braeloine Cottage is now a visitors' centre.

Less than two miles west of the Half-Way Hut on the road through the glen is Etnach, a farm near the Water of Tanar, with some farm buildings set back on the hill. There were a number of crofts there at one time — the Auld House o' Etnach, Townhead of Etnach and Waterside of Etnach. Another croft beside a pool on the Tanar was known as the Rumbling Pots. When Queen Victoria passed Etnach, or Eatnoch as she called it, she thought it 'a very lonely place'.

The old inn of Coirebhruach once stood at the foot of Mount Keen. Now only a rickle of stones are left to remind us of the days when drovers 'leap-frogged' over the hill with their cattle, when bands of young men and women plodded over the Ladder on their way to work at harvests in the south, and when Queen Victoria rode up what she called 'this curious conical-shaped hill' on one of her Great Expeditions.

*Inchrory from Ruigh Speanan.*

*The cottage at Laggan.*

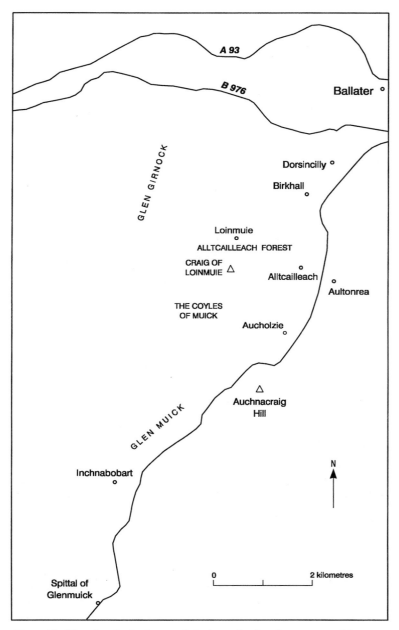

*Map 10. The 'lost' clachan of Loinmuie is shown on this map. Inchnabobort is now a Royal 'bowff' used by Prince Charles.*

# CHAPTER 10

# LOOKING FOR LOINMUI

Oh, smile for me, Loinmui fair,
Sae comely in the caller air,
For I may never see thee mair
Nor hearth nor hame nor rodden tree.

**H**idden away in the Deeside hills is a clachan that has always
had a special fascination for me. Its name — Loinmuie. It lies
below the Craig of Loinmui, one of the three tops of the Coyles of
Muick, where Alltcailleach Forest sweeps up from the valley of the
Muick and folds over it like a dark green plaid. They say that at one
time you could stand at the farm of Alltcailleach on the Birkhall road
and count more than twenty reekin' lums on those 'high and airy'
slopes. Now they are all gone.

The Deeside poet Betty Allan mirrored both the magic and sadness
of Loinmuie in her poem about leaving Glen Muick. Another
unknown poet mourned its ruined walls — 'where the thistle waves
and grass grows green' — and longed for a return to happier days when
families of Lachlans, Riachs and Dowies were seen in the old clachan.

When I went in search of Loinmuie I was looking for a fire tower
marked on a map near the site of the clachan, but it was no longer
there. A forestry worker told me it had been demolished some
twelve years ago when the trees had outgrown the tower, which
had become unsafe. Nevertheless, he knew the whereabouts of
Loinmuie — Loinmuie Farm, he called it. Most of these settlements
ended up as farms as the crofts disappeared. The forester told me
how to get there, adding that there wasn't much left of it to see.

He said that the trees around Loinmuie had been cleared only a
few weeks earlier. It was a lucky break, for if that hadn't happened
I might never have found it. It lay at the end of a long straight track
where a turning-point had been laid out for forestry vehicles.
Beyond that, light streamed through a gap in the woods — an
unexpected doorway to the past. Through it I could see dykes and
gable-ends and the shape of a settlement that had been there for
more than three centuries.

It was an exhilarating moment, but also a sobering one. Out on the hill, looking at the shattered walls of the old clachan, I remembered how Desmond Nethersole-Thompson and Adam Watson had said in *The Cairngorms* that even without evictions and clearances there would be 'empty houses and no voices on the braes'. Here, their words hung over this dead township like a shroud.

The giant root of a fallen tree lay grotesquely across one of the ruins. Tree-stumps stuck up like severed limbs. One 12 feet high trunk, shorn of its bark, still stood erect, looking down on the scene. When I saw it I thought of the verse in Adam Watson and Betty Allan's *Place Names of Upper Deeside,* written last century by a Glenmuick man before he went abroad. He had been talking his leave of his native glen and of 'Loinn Muighe, wi its aulden rodden tree'. Wandering about the old townships on Deeside, I had often came upon rowan trees planted outside cottages to ward off evil spirits. There was no trace of an 'aulden rodden tree' in the ruins of Loinmuie; maybe it, too, had been cut down.

Longhouses lay in front of me like pieces in an unfinished jigsaw. I tried to imagine the completed picture, to see what it was like in the clachan before the forest closed in on it. One house stood out from the others, its gable walls 2 feet thick, the stone clean and white, sheltered perhaps by the forest, its huge fireplace, with an alcove on either side, marking it out as the home of someone of importance. There were other houses less striking, more roughly made, and a scattering of small oval-shaped buildings. Under the grass covering the floor of one of them cobbles could be seen.

This then, was Loinmuie, where the 'thistles waved and the grass grew green', just as the old poem had said. This was where those 'happy families' had lived, 'the Lachlans, Riach and Dowie'. Dowie was an alias for Stewart, a name taken after the '45 Rising, when it was dangerous to flaunt anything with a Jacobite ring to it. It was the Stewarts who had drawn me to Glenmuick, for they were my wife's forbears, the link going back to 1681 when William Stewart, son of Thomas Stewart of Aucholzie entered into a contract of wadset (mortgage) with the Earl of Aboyne for the sale of the lands of Acholzie, Upper and Nether Achnacraig, Stodartcroft, Belino (Balnoe) and the Haugh of Acholzie.

Loinmuie was a 'lost' township when James Macdonald wrote about it in 1899 and gave its meaning as 'enclosure of the top or height'. He marked it down as 'obsolete' and added 'The place was

*Some of the ruined buildings at Loinmuie, above Birkhall in Glenmuick.*

on a hillside, close to a knoll'. When the Aberdeen naturalist
Professor William Macgillivray came upon it in 1850 it was a farm.
He had been studying the rocks 'on the south shoulder of Coial' (one
of the Coyles of Muick) and 'proceeded to Linmuic, passing the little
peak of the wooded hill above Birk Hall, about 500 paces from the
farm-house'. Sixteen years later, Captain R E Pratt carried out a
survey of Loinmuie for the first 1:60,000 Ordnance Survey map.
Nine buildings were marked on the settlement, but a cryptic entry
beside them said 'Loinmuie (In Ruins)'.

Captain Pratt's map showed that Loinmuie could be approached
from a different direction — from another 'lost' township in
neighbouring Glen Girnock. Its name was Lynhort or Linquoich and
the remains of it lay in the heather about a mile and a half up the
glen on the east side of the Girnock Burn, opposite the deserted
farm of Loinveg on the west side of the burn. The 1856 map showed
a path which branched off the Glen Girnock road, crossed the
Girnock Burn, and, skirting Lynhort, ran for about a mile directly
over the moor to Loinmuie. In the mid-19th century the township,
which is seen with a large open area around it stood near the edge
of the Alltcailleach Forest, but was eventually swallowed up by it.

The Stewarts had long links with Loinmuie. It was said that every Sunday night nineteen of them gathered at the Brig o' Muick, young blades out for a stroll, meeting to gossip and boast about their conquests, as young men do. The beginning of the clachan's decline can be seen in the Census returns and Valuation Rolls of 1841 and 1851. In 1841 there were four households — twenty-two people — in Loinmuie. The head of one of the households was John Stewart, a farmer. In 1851 there was only one household and John Stewart, now aged 51, was described as 'a farmer of 30 acres employing two servants'.

Ten years later, Loinmuie had vanished from the records. It turned up again in the Valuation Roll of 1859–60, but now it was linked with another farm-toun — Alltcailleach, which was also on the west bank of the River Muick. The entry read 'Loinmuie and Atlhallock', and the tenant was given as 'James Stewart's heirs'. Another decade on Althallock, or Altcailleach, appeared on its own. This time, Loinmuie had gone for good.

The farm of Alltcailleach lies at the foot of the vast sprawl of forest below Loinmuie. There were other townships along the river, among them Dorsincilly, now a farm but originally a clachan, with seven families living there in 1696. Also there were Crost, meaning a 'crossing', and Knok (Knock) which had twelve tenants, most of them married, including a Stewart and a Lachlan. So it was more than likely that there had been twenty reekin' lums in those 'high and airy' places at one time.

On the east bank of the Muick ruined settlements were strung out along the glen from the Brig o' Muick to the Spital...Altanzie was one; obsolete, said Macdonald. The name meant *Allt teanga*, 'burn of the tongue (of land)' and it once had seven tenants, one with his wife 'and John Elmsly, his son *in famila'*, another with the peculiar name of William M'Ondach.

Then there was Aultonrea, which became the subject of a well-known painting by the Glenmuick artist Howard Butterworth, who put on canvas the scene when the farm was up for roup a few years ago. Behind the farm you can see traces of six longhouses enclosed by a stone dyke and two kailyards. A report by Ian Shepherd, the Aberdeenshire district archaeologist, said it had possibly been abandoned in the 19th century, and added:'Earlier walls visible but robbed'. No doubt some hard-headed farmer with little respect for tradition had carted them off to make a byre or another dyke.

Perhaps the most interesting site today is Blacharrage, shown on an 1869 map as Balacariag, which was said to be 'a substantial township of twelve houses, three enclosures and a corn-drying kiln'. The kiln is still there and the sinuous pattern of run-rigs stand out quite clearly. From Blacharrage a sunken track runs on to another settlement, Loinmore, where there were five houses, Tombeck, Bealachodhar, Toldhu, Knockandbu, Rinasluick, Balendory, Balnoe...the names come echoing down the years.

Up on Auchnacraig Hill, almost opposite the Linn of Muick, a settlement that has always seemed to me to be hidden away from the outside world in a green, sheltered bowl cut off from the rest of the glen are the remains of a township consisting of five longhouses and an enclosure, with another township of four longhouses nearby. The 1696 Poll Book listed ten tenants there, seven with their wives. Looking south to Inchnabobart, once a farm, now a Royal howff for Prince Charles they would have watched the drovers pushing their black cattle across the Muick to Titaboutie, where they rested before going over the Capel Mounth to markets in the south.

On the north side of Auchnacraig Hill were the 'lands of Acholzie', which William Stewart bought in 1681; fifteen years later the Poll Book took note of 'William Stewart of Achollie his lands in the said pariochin' and recorded that he had a wife and four children, Alexander, Charles, Barabara and Elizabeth. There was a fifth still to come. The Stewarts were allied by marriage to the 'wild and extravagant' McHardies of Crathie and Crathienaird, and together they 'gave much trouble to their neighbours'.

They spread out across Deeside and into Donside. They were born, lived, worked and died in places that have either vanished or are little more than ill-remembered names...Coirebhruach, at the head of Glentanar, where the ruins of an old inn can still be seen at the foot of Mount Keen; the Stile of Tullich, with not a stone to remind us of the inn that was there; Ballaterach, the holiday home of young George Byron; the Whitestile of Pannanich the *old* Pannanich, where a handful of cottages still survive; and Etnach, on the road going west through Glentanar.

John Stewart was innkeeper and farmer at Etnach in 1776. His son, Harry, born in 1764, took over as mine host and later became innkeeper at the Stile of Tullich, a farm west of Cambus o' May, which later became a public house. Harry was twice married, the second time to Janet Cattanach, from Glenbardie, the remote glen that I had come upon while tramping across the Morven braes. Harry and Janet had a son, Charles, who was born at the Stile of Tullich in 1802. Twenty-five years later, Charles married Margaret Calder, daughter of Isaac Calder, the millwright at Greystone, Inchmarnoch. It was to Isaac's workshop that the poet Byron went as a boy when staying at Ballaterach. Margaret Calder said he was a 'tricket nickum — a very takkin' laddie, but nae easily managed'.

Ballaterach sits on the edge of moorland stretching away to Pannanich and over the Black Moss to Etnach and Mount Keen. It was there by the Pollagach Burn that Charles Stewart was killed by lightning on 8 August 1849. His son, also Charles, was for many years shepherd to the Marquis of Huntly and later to the eccentric laird, Sir William Cunliffe Brooks, who was known as WCB. He once used his initials to name a Glentanar estate road after himself — Wilcebe Road. Francis Diack recorded a place-name rhyme about the Ballaterach shepherds:

> Ballatrach's shepherds watched their sheep
> In Torrykee by nicht;
> The Caesar dog cam barkan' by
> An' put them a' to flicht.

Torrykee (*Torraidh Cithe*), 'the little hillock of mist', is south of Ballatarch. The poem goes on to say that the 'vrichtie' (millwright) turned the sheep 'an put them to Rinmore'. I have often wondered if the vrichtie was Isaac Calder, who locked the door of his workshop and went 'awe' oot aboot' when he saw young Geordie Byron approaching.

Charles Stewart, the shepherd, was born at Whitestile Pannanich. Some ten years ago I came across an old sepia portrait of him. He was wearing a plaid and bonnet, his stick and Bible on his knee and his collie dog at his feet, and on the back of the picture were the words, 'R Milne, Aboyne, Portrait and Landscape Photographer'. It put me on the trail of this little-known Deeside photographer, with the result that I wrote a series of articles for the *Press and Journal* on the forgotten man of Victorian photography.

It led to the unearthing of a treasure chest of Royal pictures. Milne was eventually appointed 'Photographer to Her Majesty in Balmoral' and took over where George Washington Wilson left off.

Charles Stewart died at Tomdarroch in 1914. His wife, Margaret Milne, died a year later. They had four children, Charles, Annie, Arthur and the oldest, Isabella, who was born at Tomdarroch in June 1856. In December 1883, 'Isie' Stewart married James McLaren from Coull. They were my wife's grandparents.

Tomdarroch was the name given to two thatched cottages in a hollow stretch of land about four miles east of Ballater on the South Deeside Road. In a document listing 'the lands and lordship of Aboyne' in 1676 it was given as Tomdorack. When my wife, Sheila, spent her school holidays at Tomdarroch as a child she played on a grassy piece of ground known as the Hillock. She didn't know then that the name Tomdarroch meant 'the hillock at the oak wood'. The name must have gone a long way back, for she has no recollection of an oak tree there.

Her grandfather, James McLaren, was a mason, a local councillor, and a man of principle. In the old days, people who set their chimneys on fire were liable to be hauled up before the local baillie and fined for their 'crime'. When Mason McLaren accidentally set *his* chimney on fire he was brought before the court in the Albert Hall in Ballater. He pleaded not guilty, pointing out that his 'lum' had been cleaned only a few days earlier. The case was thrown out and a local poet wrote a poem about it. It caused a great stir in Ballater, making James McLaren something of a local hero.

Many years ago, I tried to trace the poem, but no one remembered it or had a copy of it. Then, while researching this book, I went into the Ballater Library to ask if they would have another go at tracking down our elusive poet. It was now the age of computers. We were linked to the Aberdeenshire Library at Oldmeldrum, the keyboard rattled out its message, and a few minutes later up came the name of Charles Davidson, a railway signalman at Ballater. This was followed by the title of a book called *Deeside Lyrics*. Suddenly, a mystery that spanned a century had been solved. Inside the book was a poem entitled 'A Ballater Police Court Incident'.

The poem began by relating how Charlie had gone to the Police Court in Albert Hall to 'hear the fun'. The courtroom was crowded, but he perched himself on the window sill as the case got under way:

> The Clerk of Court 'kicked off' the ball,
> And 'Harry Calder' loud did call,
> Then read the charge: That with intent
> Accused had set fire to his vent.

The Provost asked what was his plea,
'I plead not guilty, sir,' said he.
The 'Bobbie' gied's moustache a tug,
Then whispered in the Fiscal's lug,
This roused up ire in Harry's breast,
He boldly entered his protest.
The Bar official did him tell
To keep his opinions till himsel'.
'Call the first witness', was the cry,
The Provost fixt him with his eye,
And gar't him swear wi' upraised han'
He strictly by the truth wad stan,
He said he clearly saw the flame,
Drew wife's attention to the same.
The wife was called and had nae doot
She saw baith sparks and fire come oot.
The exact position o' the can
And chimney, too, she tell't affhan'.
The witnesses for the defence
Admittit that the smoke was dense.
But it appeared to them they said,
To let oot reek the lum was made.
There was nae fire that they could see;
They were on oath and widna lee.
Noo, foo wad ye hae judged the case
Had ye been in the Provost's place?
When twa swore that the flame they saw,
And twa there was nae fire ava.
The Provost rose to the occasion,
Summed up his speech with this oration,
'Since serious doubts disturb my mind,
Not guilty, Harry, you I find.'
'Court's over!' some one loud did roar,
And ane and a' made for the door,
And doun Monaltrie Road pell-mell
To drink the hauf-croon left as bail.
We shifted twa-three pints o' ale,
Discuss't the case in each detail,
And on ae 'pint' did a' agree
That some ane must hae tellt a lee.

The name 'Harry Calder' was quoted in the poem, making it clear it was a *nom de plume*. Either Charlie Davidson had changed the name to avoid embarrassing his friend, or James McLaren had asked him to hide his identity. But there was a Harry Calder; he was one of 'Grannie' McLaren's forbears, related to the Isaac Calder of Inchmarnoch.

'Grannie' McLaren was an equally strong character. She was an inveterate bookworm — it was said that she had read every book in Ballater library — and she was acutely interested in politics, willing to cross swords with any politically-minded visitor to her home at Tomdarroch. She detested Churchill — and she was kind to the tinkers. They were old-style *tinklers,* not the much abused tinkers of later years. They came to Tomdarroch on a horse-drawn 'cairtie' full of bairns, offering to mend pots and pans and to sell 'besoms' to keep the house tidy. They lived in an open area of land at Inchmarnoch known as 'The Tinkers' Green'.

Tomdarroch was a kind of dream-world to children who stayed with 'Grannie' McLaren in the years between the wars. The sun always shone, or seemed to. The most important luggage they took on holiday consisted of a bathing costume and a parasol. There were no roses round the door at Tomdarroch, but the walls of the 'thackit hoosie' were smothered in white Morning Glory. An old-fashioned hand -pump stood at the door, drawing water from a nearby well. Turkeys gurgled and gobbled about the place, fattening themselves for Christmas. Inside, there were three box beds in the upstairs rooms, and downstairs huge pots hung from a black swey in a big open fireplace that had been painted white. The pots were for the turkeys.

There was a snowball tree at Tomdarroch, growing out of a dyke at the bottom of Grannie's garden. It was a harbinger of summer, bursting out in all its glory when June came. They thought it would last for ever. There were picnics on the Hillock and walks through the wood to Cambus o' May. The wood is shown on the map as Torphantrick Wood and in it are the ruins of farm buildings, formerly a settlement.

I went back to Tomdarroch with Sheila, the 'parasol girl' who grew up to become my wife. 'Grannie's' cottage had gone, as had its neighbour. There was no more Morning Glory. Cattle had churned up the ground, turning a once beautiful garden into a sea of mud. We sat on the Hillock, musing on how it had been all those years ago. We looked for the old path through the wood, but it had disappeared. We searched for the one thing we thought would still be there, defying the years — the snowball tree. It, too, had gone.

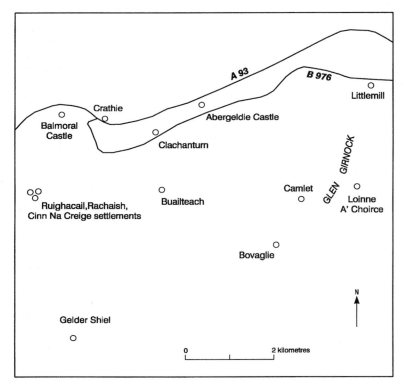

*Map 11. Ruined settlements on the Royal estate at Balmoral are seen on this map, along with townships in Glen Girnock.*

# CHAPTER 11
# HER MAJESTY'S DEER

**D**eer grazed on the grasslands of Glen Gelder. The circle of trees that sheltered Ruidh na Bhan Righ, the Queen's Shiel, lay to the west, while beyond them the black corries of Lochnagar were streaked with the last of the winter snow. From here, on the Royal estate at Balmoral, the 'burn of the clear water' begins its run to the Dee.

I was looking for Rachaish, a 'lost' community I had heard about somewhere on the banks of the Gelder. Its Gaelic name, *Ruighe Chois* pointed the way — the cattle run of the hollow. In the 'hollow' lay the ruins of not one, but three townships, half-hidden in the moorland spreading out below the glen road. Near the burn, the heather gave way to open pasture.

The old track linking the settlements was still there. The first *larach* lay on the edge of the track, then others appeared, scattered across the moor. They had been buildings of considerable size, put together with huge stones. The walls of some were 4 feet high, while others still had their gable-ends, or parts of them.

The first buildings I came to were the remains of Rachaish's neighbouring township, Ruighachail, the cattle run of the kale. I climbed on to a hillock on the edge of the grazing land. From there I could see ruins spread all over the moor. Lochnagar was a dark silhouette in the background. I could see, too, the track running on to the second township, Rachaish. I paced out the length of one longhouse there; it was 50 feet, with a 30 feet extension at one end. Not far from the burn was a large kiln.

There were said to be ten ruinous buildings at Ruighachail, four enclosures and one corn drying kiln. Rachaish was a depopulated settlement with the remains of five or more longhouses and two small enclosures, while up from Rachaish were the remains of at least two longhouses.

The old track veered away from the Gelder Burn and ran through a belt of trees east of Achadh na Creige. There, swallowed up by the woodland, was the third settlement — Cinn na Creige, smaller, but with the same big-boulder houses half-buried in the heather. Farther on were open fields and across the Gelder was Canup, where in 1862 a cairn was built to mark the wedding of the Princess Royal to Prince Frederick William of Prussia. Like most settlements, the three Gelder townships had ended up as farms.

An archaeologist's report said, 'Reason and date of depopulation unknown', but a clue to what cleared the settlements lay in a book written in 1892 by the Deeside historian, Alex Inkson McConnochie. In *The Royal Dee*, McConnochie told of meeting an 'old dame, faggot-burdened', who thought there was 'nae a Queen that I ever read o' like the Queen o' Britain'. She had only one complaint — her Majesty's deer had been coming down and eating up her turnips.

She remembered when Victoria had first come to Balmoral, and she could tell of the time when Sir Robert Gordon had the lease of the estate. Sir Robert, brother of Lord Aberdeen, became lessee in 1830 and died when a fishbone stuck in his throat. The Queen and Prince Albert took over the lease in 1848. McConnochie's garrulous old lady told him that her mother, Jean, had a small holding in Glen Gelder when Sir Robert was the laird, adding bitterly that she had to 'leave to make room for the deer'.

Although she was given a better house, old Jean threw 'a parting malediction' at Sir Robert — he would not get a stag as long as she was alive she said. The laird did, in fact, fare badly with the deer. 'Is that witch, Jean, still alive?' he would ask, but his bad luck had more to do with his poor shooting than with the old woman's prophecy. The Balmoral deer forest came into being in 1833, so it is likely that the cottars in Ruighachail and Rachaish abandoned the settlements in the 1830s.

I left the Gelder Burn, climbing out of the cattle run of the hollow, wondering where old Jean's holding had been. John Stirton, in his book, *Crathie and Braemar*, wrote about life in these old settlements. The lower classes, he said, lived in hovels built of rough boulders, similar to those I had seen at Ruighachail. They were held together by dried mud and thatched with heather or broom. These 'but and bens' were divided by a wooden partition, with an earthen floor 'often so uneven that in damp weather pools of water had to be stepped across to reach the peat fire which burned in the wide hearth'.

When Queen Victoria and Prince Albert bought Balmoral Castle, Albert thought that workers' cottages on the estate 'bordered on the Irish'. Like Stirton, he regarded many of them as 'miserable hovels' and set out to replace them. Today, it is hard to believe that Rulghachail and Rachaish ever existed.

But everything changes. Across the Dee, Crathie comes alive when the tourists arrive and the Royal family come to stay at Balmoral; in winter it goes into hibernation. Crathie was originally a small property running eastward for about a mile along the north bank of the Dee from the Mill of Crathie, opposite Balmoral Castle, to Tomidhu. Tomidhu, or Tomyadow, was a pendicle of the Crathie estate. It took its name from two heathery mounds known as the black hillocks, one of which was removed in 1979 to provide gravel for road widening.

The clachan of Milltown of Crathie was a busy place in its day, with a kirk, a manse, a glebe, and a churchyard. It had a ferry and a ford which linked Deeside with the south by the Capel Mounth and Glen Clova. Montrose, in his retreat through Angus to the north, crossed the river there in May 1645. Long after that there was a boathouse at the Milltown serving refreshments to passing travellers. In 1801 the mill had gone, although the name Milltown remained, and in time the ferry and ford fell into disuse. The boathouse was used as an inn until 1824, when it was demolished.

In 1635 there were twenty-one separate properties and eighteen different proprietors in the parish of Crathie, but in 1696, the year of the Poll Tax, there were only eleven properties, although the number of proprietors remained the same. By 1794 the number of proprietors had dropped to six.

The Crathie estate had a sizeable population in the late 17th century. The 1696 Poll Book shows that three lairds, all McHardies, had portions of it, with twelve tenants between them. John M'Hardy of Daldownie had five tenants (with wives), and two servants. One of the tenants was William Ego, the shepherd who had a Gaelic rhyme written about him. The second portioner, Edward M'Hardy, had four tenants (with wives) and two cottars, and John M'Hardie of Crathie had three tenants (also with wives), thirteen sub-tenants and two cotters. The holdings of two of his tenants were at Crathienaird and 'Tomindowies', both in the parish of Crathie.

Old valuation rolls between 1635 and 1795 throw up names of crofts and ferm touns that can still be seen today, although many now lie in ruins. Among them are Camlit (Camlet) and Bovaglia in Strathgirnock and Balnacroft at Abergeldie. The Smith's Croft of Inverzaldie was at Invergelder; Dremnapark was Drumnapark or

Druim na Pairce, south of Abergeldie, and Lynbeg was Loinveg, which I was to come across while searching for lost clachans along the Girnock Burn. Some names had become badly distorted... Chogoir was Tulach Chocaire, a croft near Tom a' Chuir south of Balmoral, and Chactanturne was Clachanturn.

Clachanturn is about a mile east of Easter Balmoral on the south side of the Dee. It once had a large and busy market and boasted an inn, a ferry and a 'smiddy'. All are gone. The name is said to be a corruption of *Clach-na—tigherna,* the laird's village. There was a school at Clachanturn about 1720 with more than eight pupils, but it was said to be broken up 'by a hellish forgery of priests and trafficking papists'.

Crathie, across the Dee, seemed to be a magnet for pipers last century, among them Alexander Downie, James Forbes, Peter Coutts, Peter Robertson and John Ross. But the King of them all was pawky Willie Blair, the Queen's fiddler, who said of his rivals that they 'hadna jist got the stott o't'. He must have moved house at some point in his career, for when he died in 1884 at the age of ninety it was at Balnacroft, where Mrs Farquharson had played host to Victoria. The house is still there today.

John Stirton thought that characters like Willie Blair would disappear with the changes taking place. He was wrong, for each generation has its own characters. I have met plenty of them in my time... people like Wullie Gray, the Bard of Corgarff, who fills the air with stories of his life as a sheep farmer, and Rab Bain, another sheep man, the last of the Gairnsiders, and Willie Forbes, a former head keeper on the Mar estate, who has built a considerable reputation as a painter and taxidermist. Willie's 19th century equivalent must surely have been a Crathie 'stuffer' known as the Professor, who lived on the north side of the Dee. Like the other Willie at Corgarff, the Professor was also a bit of a poet, but they say he was better at stuffing birds and stags' heads than he was at writing verse.

I was drawn away from Crathie, south to Glen Girnock, by another of Stirton's characters — the Minister of the Camlet. The Minister, with his 'sanctified mien and semi-clerical get-up', would have been at home in Strathgirnock, for it is a glen of ghosts, full of abandoned farms, tumbling dykes, and ruined settlements. It is remote and neglected, its past tainted with tales of witches and witch-burning.

*Camlet Settlement.*

From the distillery at Easter Balmoral a track goes south-east to Inchnabobart, on the banks of the River Muick, which drovers forded on their way over the Capel Mounth. Once a farm, it is now a luxury howff for Prince Charles. Less than a mile along the Inchnabobart road is Bualteach or Boultshoch, which was also a farm. It sits on the edge of scraggy moors that stretch away to the Muick and the corries of Lochnagar. Here, great herds of deer graze during the summer; in winter, when an icy shroud drops over the hills, I have seen keepers feeding them from carts of potatoes and hay at the side of the Bovaglia track.

Bualteach stands below a hill called Tom Bualteach, and the name tells us something about the past. It is known locally as the Tom o the Bualteich and it means 'hillock of the summer hut'. This was where the crofters came during the transhumance, the annual migration to the hills to feed their cattle on fresh summer pastures. James Macdonald was more explicit in his translation of *Builteach,* which he gave as the Gaelic for Boultschoch. He said it meant 'dairyhouses or booths' — the bothies of the cattlemen whose wives milked the cows during the summer grazing.

The Girnock track cuts away about half a mile south of Bualteach and runs down through the woods of Bovaglia. The shuttered windows of Bovaglia tell the old story; this was once a busy 'ferm toun', now it is dead and deserted. Scott Skinner, the Strathspey

*Camlet Kiln.*

King, wrote a tune called Bovaglie's Plaid, inspired by a local saying that the wood 'haps (shelters) Bovaglie ferm like a plaid'. They say that Queen Victoria heard it and gave the phrase to Ballochbuie Forest — 'the bonniest plaid in Scotland'. The remains of longhouses can be seen on the east side of the farm.

The track turns north beyond Bovaglie and here you are entering the Minister of Camlet's territory. Who he was and what connection he had with Camlet I never discovered. He saw himself as a prophet. 'This is no a lee I'm tellin' ye', he would say, but he had a furtive way of looking at you from under his eyebrows and few believed him.

The minister liked to set 'the mark of the beast' on those who scoffed at him. In some ways, he was in the right setting, for Camlet sits on a hill with a murky reputation. It was up on Creag nam Ban (the hill of the women) that witches were burned. Kitty Rankine was the last victim; one of a number of cairns on the hill is said to mark the spot where she was tied to the stake. George VI stayed at Abergeldie Castle with his brother Bertie (later Edward VIII) and they thought that its bat-infested tower was haunted by her ghost.

The farm is on top of a track that climbs up the hill from the glen road and then curves back to it in a great loop. The rocky hill behind the farm is Sgor an h-Iolaire, the peak of the eagle, but you will not see eagles there now. Yet the hills around Camlet are majestic enough for this soaring bird of prey. From the top of Creag nam Ban the face of Lochnagar seems nearer than it actually is. Clouds

*Loinveg, Girnock.*

scowled above its corries and I wondered how many Girnock folk had stood on the Witch's Hill and watched its changing moods.

Some, maybe, from the 'lost' settlements that once encircled Camlet and now lie half-buried in the heather. The remains of four longhouses can be traced immediately to the west of the farmhouse, each measuring about 10m by 3m, while two more are inside the loop. There is also a small abandoned settlement with longhouses just to the north of the track on the east side of the farm. An old lime kiln in superb condition can be seen at the roadside.

Down the glen was Loinveg, another abandoned farm. The remains of shielings can be seen there. There were as many as twenty families in Camlet in the 19th century, the last as late as 1950, and it is not so many years ago that Loinveg was occupied. Below Loinveg, across the Girnock Burn, I was looking for another 'lost' settlement. The first time I heard about it was when I was searching for Loinmuie in Glenmuick. It seemed to me then that the only approach to it was through the Alltcailleach Forest in Birkhall, but I discovered from the 1869 OS map that an old path ran across the moor from Glen Girnock and ended up in Loinmuie. This, I thought, had probably been a route linking the two communities and opening up a route into Glenmuick and over the Capel Mounth to the south.

*The ruins of Ruigbacbail on the Balmoral estate, looking towards Lochnagar.*

The path started at a group of buildings shown on the map on the east side of the Girnock Burn, almost opposite Loinveg, but neither the 1869 map or its modern equivalent put a name to it. Its name, I learned later, was Loinn a' Choirce, but there were other alternatives. One was Lynefork, otherwise the Overpleuche of Strathgirnok, meaning the upper ploughing. Loinn a' Choirce meant the field of oats, but there was nothing to suggest either oats or ploughing in the wilderness that had grown around its ruins.

The approach to it from Glen Girnock was by a path running through a small woodland almost opposite Loinveg. The path came to a halt on the edge of the Girnock Burn, but from there I could see a familiar pattern of ruined buildings in the heather across the water. A survey carried out at Loinne a' Choirce by Ian Shepherd, the Aberdeenshire archeologist, showed a settlement with different styles and dates of dwellings. Longhouses, a corn-drying kiln and the faint remains of a kailyard were found. The longhouses were turf-built and stone-built. The ruins lie on two levels, with a superb view up the glen. From the river an indistinct path climbs up to a gap in the hills, the route taken between Loinn a' Choirce and Loinmuie.

Loinveg is three miles from Littlemill, an attractive hamlet at the mouth of Glen Girnock, where a road goes west from the Brig o'

*From Gelder Shiel, looking towards Lochnagar.*

Muick to Balmoral. Prince Albert opened a school at the Bridge of Girnock, as well as at Crathie and Birkhall. Before the Girnock track runs out the Mill of Cosh can be seen on the right, its waterless wheel silent and unused.

Across the track, another woodland 'haps' the remains of Glen Girnock's last settlement — Na Cearr-lannan, which like many other small clachans was known as the Street. There were two rows of houses in this Street made from stones and divots and built into the lower slopes of Craig Ghiubhais.

Between the Girnock and Gelder burns lies a great skelp of Royal land reaching out to Lochnagar and Loch Muick. Strathgirnock was notorious for its illegal uisquebhaugh. The whisky-makers cocked a snook at the gaugers in this quiet glen; there were no fewer than eleven 'black bothies' (illicit stills) in the upper part of the glen.

Glen Gelder, on the other hand, was nearer to Balmoral and more open to the public. Today, hillwalkers, starting at Easter Balmoral, make a beeline for the Gelder Shiel — Ruidh na Bhan Right. Members of the Royal Family still picnic and barbecue there, just as Queen Victoria did, but the stables have been given over as a bothy for hillwalkers and climbers.

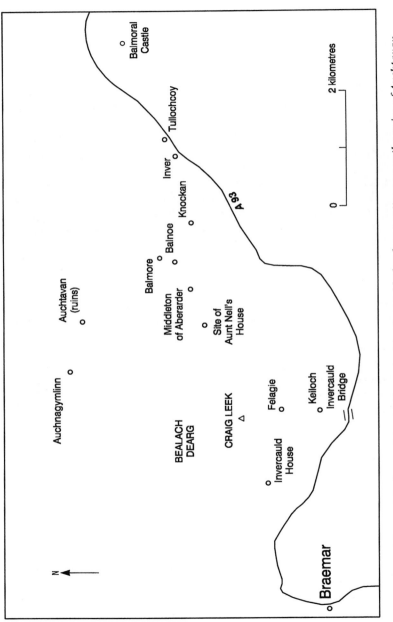

Map 12. *The vanished townships in Aberarder. The Queen Mother has a cottage near the ruins of Auchtavan.*

# CHAPTER 12
# LAND OF LOST CONTENT

The clouds were dancing a reel in the corries of Lochnagar, blown by a wind that rattled the rooftops of Tullochcoy. 'What does the name mean?' I asked Colin Fraser, the farmer. 'The windy hill', he said. Tullochcoy, *tulach-gaoith*...the 'windy knoll' was how the place-name experts translated it. It was more than a knoll, as I discovered when I tramped up the long, steep brae that led to the farmhouse. Up there, you seem to be standing on the edge of the world.

Tullochcoy looks much like any other hill farm. It had been a bad winter, with a lot of frost, water streaming down the hill. Now glaur caked the rutted farm tracks. It was the lambing season. Colin was away tending to the 'yowes', but his son, Bruce, who works on a farm at Peterhead, was at home helping his father. Colin, a shepherd's crook in his hand, turned up later.

Colin's father and grandfather were at Tullochcoy before him. Today, like so many other farms, it has virtually become a one-man business, with Colin's wife, Pat, who works in a Deeside tourist office, helping out, Bruce pitching in when he is at home, and someone coming in to lend a hand when needed.

Yet this windy farmtoun was once a small estate with twenty people living and working on it. In the Poll Book of 1696 the property is shown under the name of Ludowick (or Lewis) Farquharson, who was 1st Laird of Auchindryne. He was the elder brother of James Farquharson, who is entered as heritor. James, who had a wife and three sons, James, David and John, became the 1st Laird of Tullochcoy. There were six tenants and their families on the estate including Jannet Allan, a widow and 'fermor'; and one sub-tenant, plus two servants.

Bruce Fraser showed me a large stone, a lintel, lying In the farmyard. It carried the inscription 'I.F.A.O. 1693'. That was three years before the Poll. It was also the date on which the mansion house of Tullochcoy was built by James Farquharson. The A.O. on the lintel stone were the initials of Agnes Ochterlony, a daughter of the minister of Fordoun.

Pat Fraser, who is interested in the history of Tullochcoy, thought that there had been a castle where the farm buildings now stand,

*Colin Fraser, the farmer at Tullochcoy.*

but it is more than likely that this was the 1693 mansion house, which was partly rebuilt in the beginning of the 19th century. The estate is said to have been in the hands of the Farquharson family for at least eighty years. It was sold by James Farquharson's great-grandson, Peter, in 1772. Peter Farquharson retired and left Deeside to live in Belnaboddach in Glenbucket, where, by a curious coincidence, Colin Fraser's grandfather farmed before coming to Tullochcoy.

The old lintel stone isn't the only link with the Tullochcoy of the past. There are ruins everywhere. The foundations of buildings can be seen on the track up to the farm as well as around it. Pat Fraser said that the foundations of many buildings could be seen in the woods under Craig Nordie, the hill behind Tullochcoy. From the farm a track runs up to the remains of the farm of Balnalan, while across the fields the broken walls of Stronagoar are scattered across the hill slopes.

Lochnagar frowned across the Dee at us. It seemed to be more magnificent, more imperious, every time I saw it from these Deeside hills. We looked towards Glen Gelder. 'They cleared them out of there', said Pat. 'They've a lot to answer for.' Creag na Spaine, with a fire track running over its brow, towered above the entrance to Aberarder, the old kirk of Knockan at its feet. The glen stretched away to Craig Leek. To the north lay Glen Fearder and the road to Auchtavan, where the Queen Mother has a 'howff'.

The lands of Aberarder, lying in the valley of the Fearder Burn, are pitted with the ruins of old settlements, crumbling reminders that this was once a well-populated area, not the bare, deserted landscape it is today. It was Donald Grant, whose father was innkeeper at Inver in the 1920s, who told me of the ruined settlements at Tullochcoy. Aberarder is Donald's 'land of lost content'. It was, he says, 'where I spent the best days of my life'. He has an album of photographs showing Aberarder as it was when he took his school holidays there with his Auntie Nell (Helen Bain). His father moved from the Inver to Fochabers in 1932 to be host at the Grant Arms, but young Donald still went on holiday to his Auntie Nell's 'hoosie' in this remote Invercauld glen.

His grandfather, Francis Grant, was gamekeeper to Sir William Cunliffe-Brooks, the laird of Glentanar. Donald himself, who ran a garage at Cullen and later became the owner of two shops, worked as a ghillie at Glentanar after he retired. He has a holiday cottage at Inchmarlo, near Banchory, but his thoughts are never very far from Aberarder.

I set off with Donald on a journey of rediscovery...up from the Inver to Felagie, passing the abandoned mission kirk, which is all that is left of the hamlet of Knockan. The church became a school and ended up as a hay store; now its doors and windows are boarded up. For a long time the kirk bell still hung from the belfry, but it eventually disappeared. From Knockan there are three roads to choose from, the first is a well-made track going south-east by Felagie and Keiloch, joining the main Deeside road near the Old Invercauld Bridge, and the second cuts away from the Keiloch road, crosses the Felagie Burn, and goes north by Balnoe and Ratlich and on to Auchtavan or over the east flank of Culardoch to the Gairn. The third takes you through the clachan of Middleton of Aberarder to Am Bealach, a high pass leading to the Bealach Dearg.

The Felagie Burn rises under Craig Leek and meanders lazily eastward towards the Fearder Burn. Its name comes from *feith leaghadh,* meaning a 'slow burn' — a bog stream — passing through land that is wet and marshy. Cattle graze there and red deer come down from the hills to feed in the glen, or to get their winter fodder from the Invercauld keeper, but parts of it can be treacherous. Donald lost his dog in this bogland when he was a boy and sheep have been sucked into its quagmires…deep holes, they say, that can swallow you up.

Looking down the Aberarder glen I was seeing two worlds; one in the past, with every house occupied and the air alive with 'voices on the brae', with peat smoke spiralling into the sky and the kirk bell at Knockan sounding out across the moors; the other was in the present with the old bell silenced and nothing but broken walls and broken dreams. The remains of the first local school can be seen across the moor on the road to Middleton of Aberarder, on the north side of Felagie Burn. In 1810 there were no fewer than 128 pupils in Aberarder, 88 boys and 40 girls. Up to the 1830s it fluctuated, with 62 in 1821 and 98 in 1834, but in the latter years of the century it dropped to an average of between 20 and 30 pupils.

On our way down the track Donald pointed to a ruin on the hill above the school. There had been a smiddy and a croft there and the people who lived in it were called Leys. John Brown's mother, Margaret Leys, was the daughter of a blacksmith at Aberarder and it was more than likely that these were the ruins of her home. There were other ruins nearby and it was only later that I learned that they were the Crofts of Balnoe, sometimes known as the Crofts of Aberarder. They are shown on the 1869 Ordnance Survey map.

Heavy woodland ran along the edge of the track to Middleton of Aberarder. Donald said that when he was a boy the trees were well back from the road. The ruins of buildings and moss-ridden dykes could be seen inside the wood. Half-way towards Craig Leek the rough track had been widened to provide a huge loading bay for timber. That was where Auntie Nell's house had been. Not a stone remained, nothing to show that anyone had ever lived there. Donald felt bitter about it. In his photograph album there is a picture of the

*Auntie Nell's house at Aberarder.*

cottage and a caption below it saying that the laird of Invercauld had razed it to the ground setting it on fire, and beside it is the message; 'Don't forget the Clearances!'

Donald walked across the gravelly timber bay, stirring the dust with his foot as if trying to unearth some link with his childhood days. The fire had consumed a period of his life when all the wonders of the world had been at his feet. Robertson's 'parkie', a cry-back to the croft that was there before Auntie Nell moved in, was at the foot of her house. In front of us the Felagie Burn ran past on its way to join the Fearder Burn. Donald had fished and taught himself to swim in that narrow, winding stream. He remembered Auntie Nell's cottage. It had a box bed in the living room and another in the sitting room and upstairs there were two bedrooms. There were no 'mod cons', no electricity or gas; the light came from candles. Nor was there any water; they got that from a well behind the house. We searched for the old 'wallie' but there was no trace of it.

*Donald Grant on the site of his Aunt Nell's house at Aberarder.*

There were other cottages at Middleton of Aberarder. They have all gone now, but the pictures in Donald's album showed what was there before the bulldozers swept them away...the heap of stones that was Bella Catnoch's house, next to Auntie Nellie's cottage; the broken gable-end of Lizzie MacHardy's house ('what *they* left of it', said the caption); the inside of the shell that had been Maggie Lamont's house, with its 'winky' window on the gable wall and weeds choking the floor; and another abandoned building, set against the background of Craig Leek, where tinkers had stayed.

The tinkers were Jeannie and Willie and the deserted building they took as their own was known as Milne's house. Jeannie and Willie would live there for a month and then move on, sometimes taking up 'residence' in the empty house, now also a ruin, near Gairnshiel Bridge, opposite the Teapot Cottage where Queen and Princess Margaret played as children. Donald knew the tinkers well, remembering how they came to the Inver Inn when his father was there. After Willie died, Jeannie ended up at the 'model' in Elgin, but she would sometimes come back to her old haunts at Aberarder. Donald would give her lunch at the inn.

So that was Middleton. The 'voices on the brae' had been stilled long before our coming, but Donald Grant, who spent 'the best years of his life' there, still held them in his memory, and in his imagination could still see the peat smoke drifting down the glen to the windy heights of Am Bealach. Auntie Nellie's garden was on the east side of the cottage. Here, a fallen tree with bleached branches and trunk lay over what had been the vegetable patch, and on the west side a lone birch tree stood beside a dyke — the 'birkie' where Donald wanted his ashes scattered, The ashes of his mother and father, his sisters and his Auntie Nell had been scattered there.

Behind the 'birkie' the moor stretched away to the Felagie road and Alltcailleach Forest. There was no woodland there when Donald was a boy. Beyond that the dark outline of Lochnagar rose above the forest — an unusual view of Byron's mountain. Across the Dee were the Woods of Garmaddie and the vast sprawl of the Royal estate. Donald's mother, Annie, and his Auntie Nell knew Balmoral well; they both worked there for Queen Victoria. They were 'skivvies', said Donald, who thought little of the way they were treated. On their week-end day off they had to walk all the way from Balmoral to Dalmochie, east of Ballater, where they had a house. The ancient ferry, the Boat of Dalmochie, operated between Tullich and Pannanich, but was unable to cope with the traffic after the 'miracle' wells.

There were a number of houses at Felagie, on the Alltcailleach side of the glen…Archie Duncan's house was there, as was Annie Mathieson's. The foundations can still be seen, but not much more. One house, however, has survived the years, although it has been modernised and turned into a Girl Guides' hut. This was where Jean and Willie Cattanach lived in the 1920s. Willie was a keeper on the Invercauld and Jean was something of a character; a kindly soul, says Donald, but never one to mince her words. When a visitor to her home in Felagie asked her where the toilet was she said, 'Go out the door, cross the moss, and turn your arse to Craig Leek'. She had eleven of a family and Donald Grant told me what happened on one occasion when the minister called. Jean asked if he would like a brew-up and when she went through to the kitchen he waited in the living room.

Sitting there, he took a look at a photograph on the mantelpiece and shouted through, 'I'm just admiring your picture on the mantelpiece, Mrs Cattanach. Is that all your family?'

'Na, na!' came the reply 'Twa o' them didna belong tae Willie.'

A narrow, mossy path runs across the moor from Felagie to where a flagpole and bits of an old rifle range can be seen at the foot of

*Jean Cattanach outside her cottage at Keiloch.*

Am Bealach. The ruins of a house stand on a knoll to the left and a short distance away a stream comes downhill to join the Felagie Burn. Here, a ford marked on the map was used by local people when they crossed the moor to the south side of the glen. They came from two old settlements which lie on the steep slopes of the Pass.

As you climb up under Craig Leek you come to a heap of stones on higher ground. They are from the 'steening' (stone clearing) of the land by crofters. Piles of them can be seen scattered on various parts of the hill. Bear left over a grassy hollow towards a line of trees on the ridge ahead and you come to an area that was once well cultivated. Here, the ruins of old holdings run hard into the gut of Am Bealach, sprawling uphill towards the road to the Bealach Dearg.

The two settlements were known as Upper and Lower Balloch, from 'bealach', a pass or hill crossing, and in the higher settlement the clear line of a street can be picked out, with houses on either side. Some of the ruins lie on the opposite side of the stream which runs down through the settlements to Felagie Burn. Surveys by the Royal Commission for Ancient and Historic Monuments of Scotland showed the foundations of a depopulated township of about 46 buildings, eight small enclosures and two corn-drying kilns. The reason for the depopulation is believed to be the introduction of sheep in the early 19th century.

Donald Grant discovered that in Aberarder in 1700 there was a shoemaker called Macpherson, while in Balloch there were two weavers, Donald Coutts and John Duncan, and a crofter, John McIntosh. An old Invercauld map showed that 'The Cyards' lived in Lower Balloch at one time. These may have been wool-carders who went about the country taking work. They were known as 'cairders', or, colloquially, 'cyaards', like the Cyaarders of Cyaak (New Pitsligo) in Buchan. On the other hand, a caird was a travelling tinker, so Donald Grant's tinker friends, Jeannie and Willie, may have been following an old tinker tradition when they came to Aberarder.

I wandered about the ruins, a patchwork of walls and gaping doorways, some with their lintels still intact. It had been a busy, lively community, hidden away from the world; now it was a crofting ghost town. I marvelled at the outlook they must have had from their township, an eagle's eye view of the glen below and the surrounding hills. Craig Leek is said to be one of the finest view-points in the district. From it you look across Aberarder to Lochnagar and the Stuic, where time stands still and nothing ever changes.

Up above the Balloch settlements a track curves away towards the Bealach Dearg, but I was going back the way I had come, past Middleton of Aberarder to the road that runs north by Balnoe and Balmore. These two farms were ruinous when I saw them, although sheep were being dipped at Balmore. Beyond Balmore the track crosses the Fearder Burn and climbs through a woodland until it comes to a fork, one track going on by the old drove road by Culardoch to Loch Builg and Tomintoul, the other turning west into Glen Fearder. Less than half a mile from the fork the ruins of an isolated croft can be seen on the hill to the north. This is, or was,

*Ruins of the old thatched cottar houses at Auchtavon, where the Queen Mother has a cottage.*

Loin, a name which simply means an enclosure. Old papers show it as Loynacoy or Line of Tullochcoy, which suggests a link with the original estate of Tullochcoy, and rental documents of 1772 give it as 'The Loin, now waste, John McPherson, the last Tenant, removed from it Whitsenday last'.

The track runs through an opening in a dyke marking the start of the Auchtavan lands. Auchtavan was at one time a fair-sized farming township. Behind another dyke that runs parallel with the road to the farm are the remains of the old settlement, ruin after ruin, set high on the brae. There is a well-preserved corn kiln on the south side of the dyke and a scattering of other ruins on the open field running down to the Fearder Burn.

Jock Esson was a shepherd at Auchtavan — and the last person to live and work there. Jock, whose son Ian runs a sheep farm at Wester Micras (see Chapter Eight), could never have imagined that Auchtavan would one day become a Royal hideaway for the Queen Mother.

Donald Grant knew Jock well. He often got a cup of tea from him, but he never drank it from a cup. 'It was all out of a bowl', said Donald, a white bowl in the old-fashioned away. The roofless shells of a number of .black houses can be seen near the Queen Mother's cottage at Auchtavan. One building did have a roof, made of corrugated iron, but this was blown off and a second roof was exposed — an old 'thackit' roof.The chimney pot had also suffered from the Fearder gales. It was made of wood, as was the 'hingin' lum' inside the house.The use of peat in the days of 'hingin' lums' made them reasonably safe.

In recent years the Queen Mother has rarely used her Auchtavan cottage, but it is kept in good order. It is the highest farm in the glen and its name means 'the field of the two kids', an indication that the rent paid to the laird of Invercauld was two young goats. Higher up the glen there was another place that was originally the highest farm in the glen. It was Auchnagymlinn, whose name sounds as forbidding as the moorland around it. It comes, in fact, from the Gaelic *Ach nan Comh-iomlaidean,* meaning 'field of the inter-changing'. In other word, runrig lands.

It has been described as 'a place long extinct'. It was destroyed by sand and gravel in the floods of 1829, washed away in the Muckle Spate, leaving behind only a rickle of stones and a fanciful tale about a giant, the last of his race, who had lived there. If you want proof of this, look for a grave about twenty-feet long somewhere above Auchnagymlinn. I never found it. Nor was I able to find any trace of runrig cultivation, although the ruins of the farm buildings are still there.

Fearder was known as the glen or bog of the high water, so it is not surprising that Auchnagymlinn was wiped out in the Muckle Spate. It says something about the conditions people had to endure in these remote settlements in those far-off days. It must have taken giants of men to carve a living out of the dour, unfriendly land, and if they were not 20 feet in height they were certainly taller than most ordinary mortals.There was, according to tradition, a family in the forks of the Fearder Burn who were all 7 feet tall — and they all died young.That, at anyrate, is another story that has drifted down the years from the glen of the high water.

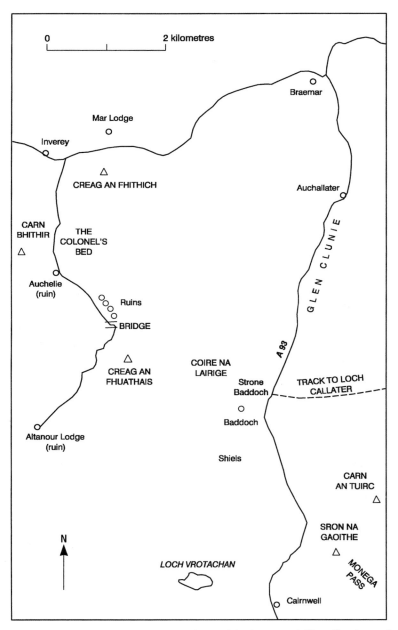

*Map 13. This map shows sheils in the Baddoch, west of Glen Clunie, and ruined settlements in Glen Ey.*

# CHAPTER 13
# GLEN OF THE FATTENING

The old Monega Pass runs across the high lands that rise above the Cairnwell road south of Braemar. It crosses the spine of Sron na Gaoithe, skirts Glas Maol, brushes the lip of Caenlochan Glen, and drops down to Glen Isla. I remember the first time I went over the ancient Pass, the highest public footpath in the country. Starting from the Sean Spittal Bridge, I forded the Allt a' Gharbh-choire and climbed up Sron na Gaoithe to pick up the track near its summit. There were old shielings — the Shielings of Coire Bhuth — on the banks of the Gharbh-choire as well as along the Allt Coire Fionn - Shiels of the Sron. They were all ruinous reminders of the days when cattle were driven there to feed on the summer pastures below the Cairnwell. They can still be seen from the Braemar-Glenshee road.

In October 1861, Queen Victoria and Prince Albert sat on the edge of the north corrie of Caenlochan and ate a picnic lunch. It was, she said, 'a very precipitous place, which made one dread any one's moving backwards', but she marvelled at 'the wonderful panorama which lay stretched out before us'. On their way up to that vast tableland the Royal party crossed the Coire Bhuth grazings, which 'included all the corries from Cairnaglasha (Cairn of Claise) round to the Cairnwell'. They came down by the Gharbh-choire Bridge, and made for home by the Sean Spittal Bridge, 'along the new road'.

In 1705, Coire Bhuth, or Corrievu, was the scene of a dispute between the Earl of Mar and the Laird of Invercauld over grazing rights. When Charles Gordon of Abergeldie was chosen as arbiter and came out in favour of Invercauld, the Earl of Mar sent a letter to him complaining about the decision. 'The Corivows were alwise in use to be driven', he wrote. 'To make a long tale short, Charles, this affair is past redding (solving) espeatially considering their justifieng the thing, and either they or I shall be master, for I'm wearie liveing betwixt hawk and bussard. You may choise as a nighbour wch to join with — Invercald or I, and I shall be glad to know yr choise you make for yr. self.'

The days of the shielings have long since gone...there are no more cattle drives, no 'hawk and buzzard' disputes, no squabbles over marches and rights of grazing. Nearly 300 years ago, after the Earl of Mar had argued about Invercauld's right to drive his cattle 'to the Corivows', sheep, not cattle, graze on the high lands where the old Monega Pass once pushed its way south. Forty years ago, a twelve-year-old girl called Winnie Cooper slept in a tent on the Corrievu pastures in the same way that youngsters had slept in the shielings when their families migrated to the hills for the summer grazing.

Winnie was there with her uncle, Jimmy Cooper, who had driven his sheep to Corrievu from the farm of Ord, near Rhynie, which he ran with his brother Robbie, Winnie's father. She had a friend with her for company — and a pet goat. In the old days the women and children milked the cows for their husbands, but Winnie milked her goat. Her uncle, however, had no taste for goat milk and had to settle for a tin of Carnation milk. The goat was tethered outside the tent, but during the night it kicked up such a row that it had to be taken inside to share the tent with the girls. Today, Winnie Cooper single-handedly runs two farms at Ord. Her father died in 1975 and her Uncle Jimmy in 1981.

One of the hills on the Monega plateau is Carn an Tuirc, some-times known simply as the Turk. Behind it are the cliffs of Loch Kander, where a path runs down to Loch Callater. Here, the ruins of shielings can be seen on the nearby burns, but high above the loch is a different kind of shiel, clinging to the rocks of Corrie Kander. If Monega is the highest public footpath in the country, this old shiel must be the highest bothy. It was seen by Professor William MacGillivray, the well-known naturalist, when he wandered over the Glas Maol plateau. He called it 'a very neat hut', with a place for a small fire, two stone benches and two recesses for pipes and other articles.

The shiel is roofless now, but one of the benches is still there, as well as the hole in the wall where the shepherd kept his pipes. From this crumbling bothy you look across the Cairnwell to where the hills stretch west as far as the eye can see. The Ordnance Survey map shows a path dropping down from Carn Aosda, north of the Cairnwell, to a hut not far from Loch Vrotachan.

Seton Gordon said that the name Vrotachan meant the Loch of the Fattening, which he thought may have come from 'the fat trout which are found in it'. In the 1793 Statistical Account for Scotland, the Rev Charles M'Hardy wrote about Loch Vrotachan being well stored with 'large delicate red trout'. Even so, it could hardly merit the title of Loch of the Fattening. On the other hand, the land below the loch could well have been called the Glen of the Fattening, for this is the Baddoch, where for centuries cattle were fed and fattened on the rich summer pastures between Glen Ey and Glen Clunie. Jimmy Cooper took his sheep to the Baddoch as well as to Corrievu. He slept in an abandoned farmhouse, although there were times when he had a less comfortable billet. Once, taking his flock home to the Ord at Rhynie and unable to find shelter for the night, he lay down where he stood, on the ground. Next morning he woke up to find himself white from head to toe, covered in frost.

The Strone Baddoch is where you enter the glen. The Strone (the name means a nose) is a prominent hillock rising up where the Baddoch Burn meets the Clunie Water. Drovers came east over the Bealach Bhuide, the Yellow Pass, from Loch Callater to the Baddoch. Near the Strone there is an old wooden gate by the roadside where hillwalkers leave their cars when walking through the Baddoch to Glen Shee. A stile takes you over the gate, a bridge over the Clunie, and the road to Baddoch beckons you towards the distant hills.

The hills by the Strone close in as you follow the track to Baddoch farm. It is a gaunt, forbidding two-storey house that looks as if it might have been built for some gloomy Victorian film set. Perhaps it was the dour grey sky and the rain that came slanting down the glen that coloured my first impression of it. The farmyard was sodden, pea-soup thick with mud. Two horses, grey to match the weather, splashed towards me, hoping for a titbit. The windows of the house were boarded up or torn out, one with a window frame hanging askew and about to fall. Roof slates had crashed to the ground, giving up the hopeless struggle. Inside was dust and decay; empty whisky bottles were dumped in the porch, an old swey that had once held bubbling pots of hot soup hung in the fireplace, two armchairs sat in front of the fire and a once-elegant cane chair had been pushed into a corner. I wondered if Jimmy Cooper had sat in it after herding his sheep on the Baddoch moors.

The outside door was a dull, faded red. There was a nameplate on it, Baddoch, and below it was the outline of a horseshoe that someone had nailed up for luck. But the horseshoe had gone and the luck with it. The Gaelic name of the farm was *A'Bhacach,* the

*Baddoch Farm.*

place of clumps. There were other farms in the Lower Baddoch, two linked by their names, Ach nan Saighdear, the field of soldiers, and Leathad nan Saighdear, the slope of soldiers, but what tale lay behind them is lost in the past.

Rienluig — Ruighe an Luig, the cattle run of the hollow — was the name of a farm west of the Strone, but the word 'Ruighe' suggests that it may have been a shieling, or a shieling that developed into a farm. In 1733 there was an unsuccessful attempt to evict tenants of the Reinluig settlement — 'to flit and remove yourselves Wives bairns families Servants Subtenants Cottars and Grassiers goods and gear.'

Shielings dominated the glen - *A'Bhadach,* the place of the clumps. Clumps and hillocks. There was a shiel by the Gairn south-east of Ben Avon known as Ruighe Bad Thomaidh, the 'shiel of clump of the little hillock'. Shielings were often sited on natural morainic hillocks or banks. If these were not available massive boulders and rock were incorporated into the construction of the shiels. The Baddoch shiels were sited on knolls near the Baddoch burn, where the ground seems to swell and dip in an endless succession of mounds and hollows; the 'clumps', presumably, of *A'Bhadach.*

*Ruined shiel in the Baddoch.*

The ruins of shiels were everywhere, on and on as I went through the glen. In a paper written for the *Proceedings of the Society of Antiquaries* in 1986, John Smith of the Department of Geography at Aberdeen University, commented on the intensity of shielings in the Baddoch. It suggested, he said, 'an intensive and carefully organised use of its "moorgrass and fine pasture". There were shiels of different shapes and sizes, some round, some rectangular, ranging from small buildings of 4 metres by 3 metres to longhouses three or four times that size. The Baddoch shiels were comparable in size to those in other parts of Deeside and Donside, or in other parts of the country. Towards the end of the 18th century there were shielings in Atholl which were about 30 feet long.

Walking through this glen of shielings, thinking of what life must have been like there, I remembered how the Inverness editor Duncan Campbell (see Chapter Four) had described the annual trek to the shielings — the small flitting, when men went up to repair and thatch the huts, and the great flitting — *Latha dol do'n ruigh* — when the women and the milk cows migrated. Children and dogs went crazy. Even the horses were affected. 'Milk vessels, churns, cheese presses, pots, pans, meal bags, salt arks, rennet apparatus, blankets, clothing, shoes and stockings — which were little used — spinning wheels, spindles and distaffs, flax and wool, with many other things, had to be packed in the light peat carts, which looked like big baskets on low wheels, that sure-footed horses could almost haul anywhere.'

The shieling lads could milk the cows and goats, but they looked upon that as women's work. The women, old and young, were 'the busy bees of the shieling hives'. Milking, cheese-making, butter-making, took the first place in their programme, and after that came the spinning of flax and wool, with other accompaniments such as the bleaching of last year's webs, the gathering of roots, herbs, backs and lichen for dyeing, and of other plants for medicinal purposes.

The Baddoch wriggles its way through great grassy hills, running out just to the west of Loch Vrotachan. The track had been widened and extended when I was there, for deer hunters, not for hillwalkers like myself. From the head of the burn a wide grassy col, peaty in places, went through to the head of Glen Ey, where the great mass of Beinn Iutharn Bheag and Beinn Iutharn Mhor dominates the landscape. Climbers tackling the Ben Uarns, as they are called, use the route through the Baddoch, returning by Glen Ey. There is another way into Glen Ey from the Baddoch. At one time, drovers coming over the Bealach Bhuide from Loch Callater went west to the Ey Burn by Coire na Lairige, the corrie of the hill pass, near the Strone.

Glen Ey has always seemed to me to be a melancholy glen, its hills scarred by bulldozed tracks, the old shooting lodge at the head of the glen in ruins, crumbling into dust in the middle of a wood whose trees have either toppled to the ground or been stripped bare by the winds off the Ben Uarns — the 'mountains of hell'. Coille Phiobair, the wood of the piper is the same, shorn of its birch trees like a sheep shorn of its wool, while near it lie the remains of Dail name Fiadh, or Dalnafae, whose people were evicted in the mid-1800s. Skeleton trees and skeleton townships...never has desolation been more evident than in this forgotten glen.

Inverey itself was described early last century as 'destined for the abode of wretchedness', its roofs composed of clods supported on rafters. 'The floor is naked earth', it was said, 'smoke and darkness prevail within'.

The Deeside writer, Alex Inkson McConnochie said in the dying years of last century that although Inverey had been described by writer after writer as 'an excellent example of a Highland clachan', it was, in fact, 'a poverty-stricken hamlet composed of miserable-looking huts'. There are actually two Invereys — Meikle Inverey, on the east side of the Ey burn, and Little Inverey on the west. The houses in Meikle Inverey are all on the north side of the road running through the village, but the foundations of earlier houses can still be seen on the south side. 'The old thatched biggins that afforded us shelter in our early wanderings have disappeared', wrote McConnochie in 1889.

Five years earlier the 'thackit hoosies' could still be seen. In 1895, there were twelve houses in Muckle Inverey. Some were slated, but three or fur of the old thatched ones remained. There was about the same number of houses in Little Inverey, five of which were thatched, four or five slated, and some of the others in ruins. One of the houses that gave hillwalkers shelter in McConnochie's time is still there — Thistle Cottage, home of the legendary Maggie Gruer, who gave shelter to hundreds of hillwalkers and climbers over the years, charging them a shilling for bed and breakfast, sixpence if they were hard up.

Not far from Maggie's old house, now a holiday home, stands another boarded-up cottage, the Mains, looking neglected and in need of paint and plaster. This was once the home of Charlie Stewart, one of my wife's forbears. Maggie was known as the Queen of Inverey, but Charlie was King. John Stirton mentioned him in his book *Crathie and Braemar*, but said that he was nicknamed 'The Princie', not the King. According to Stirton he was the last of the illicit whisky-makers.

When you leave Inverey and head up the glen, past what is left of the Mill of Inverey and the line of the old mill lade, past the site of the miller's house and the sheep pens, over the wooden Ey brig and on up the brae, Cnoc Chadail, the sleepy hillock lies ahead. It is said that a man was tempted into it by the fairies and when he came out seven years later he found that his bairns had grown up. Beyond Cnoc Chadail is Carn Bhithir, the ridge of the high point. A long time ago someone wrote a Gaelic rhyme about Carb Bhither, telling of a lazy man who reluctantly tore himself away from his fireside to go up the hill to collect his peats:

> My black little heap of peats
> On the top of Carn a' Bhir,
> In the cold of a winter's night
> I've got to go and seek them.

Glen Ey is full of such stories. A bulldozed track runs above the old way up the glen and it was from there that William Macgillivray looked south and saw 'a fair green strath, smooth as a well-kept lawn...as beautiful as an English park'. That was in 1855, not many years after the glen had become depopulated, but before the townships had begun to disintegrate.

Macgillivray saw that the hillsides had been 'burnt in wide spaces which are now covered with verdure', but, he added, 'all around not a single sheep is to be seen'. About 1840, nine farming clachans in Glen Ey were wiped out by local clearances. The old Highland black cattle had been replaced by sheep, and now, in turn, the sheep were replaced by deer; human beings had become redundant. Today, hundreds of deer winter in Glen Ey on what was once fertile crofting land.

I saw great herds of them on the mountain ridges when I went through the glen. There are names that recall the days when cattle and sheep filled the glen, others that remind us that now the deer hold sway. Allt nan Laogh, east of Altanour, means the burn of the calves, and Glacan Poll Smloraich, also on the east side of the glen, means the 'little hollow of sheep-dipping'. Coire nam Fiadh, high above the point where a bridge crosses the Ey, is the corrie of the deer, and it was there that I saw the last of the stags as I went on to the ruined shooting lodge.

South of the Colonel's Bed, the rocky shelf where the Black Colonel, John Farquharson of Inverey, hid from the Redcoats, a large area of grassland spreads across the hillside, with more on the other side of the track, dropping down to the Ey. This is part of the 'fair green strath' that William Macgillivray saw. It is dissected by long lines of broken dykes. Inside them are the ruins of homes that gave Glen Ey its reekin' rums. At Achery, in one corner of Macgillivray's 'wide spaces', are two ruined buildings which date from more recent times.

Heaps of rubble and the foundations of houses and out buildings lie on either side of the Ey, their names almost forgotten...Ruintellich, Dalruinduchlat, Allshlat, Garnafea, Dalrafae, Rido. The glen is peppered with old dykes, the outlines of buildings, stone clearance heaps, cornkilns and limekilns, and even the flagstones that in some houses covered the floors. Dalruinduchlat was occupied by Lamonts from the early 19th century and it was a Calum Lamont who is said to have had the Piper's wood named after him.

I was thinking of another Lamont when I was there — Kate Lamont, Ceitidh Chaluim, one of the last surviving natives of Glen Ey, who was a friend of Jean Bain, the mother of Rab Bain from the Ardoch at Crathie. Jean Bain was brought up at Inverey. Just as Mrs Bain had given information on the Gaelic to Adam Watson and Betty Allan, so Kate Lamont was a valuable source of information on folklore, proverbs, stories, and place-names to Francis Diack, author of *Place-Names of the North-Eastern Highlands*.

Kate had a fine turn of phrase. Diack wrote down many of her sayings. 'If I had teeth of my own', she would say, 'they would be shaking in my gob with the cold', or, commenting on some taciturn acquaintance, she would remark, 'I thought sometimes you would have to take the tongs to get the words out of him'. Diack, who obviously required no tongs for Kittie Calum, drew up a list of minor names in Glen Ey, 'beginning at Creag an fhithich and returning to it'. Creag an Fhithich is east of the Ey Burn, overlooking Meikle Inverey.

Creag an Fhuathais is a dark, dome-like hill that towers above the Ey Burn, guarding the pass that runs the last two miles to Altanour and the old shielings beyond it. Meoir Ghrianaich, the sunny stream, is in sharp contrast to it, for in both name and appearance Creag an Fhuathais is a forbidding peak. Diack said its name meant 'dreadful craig', and Adam Watson translated it as the 'cliff of the spectre'.

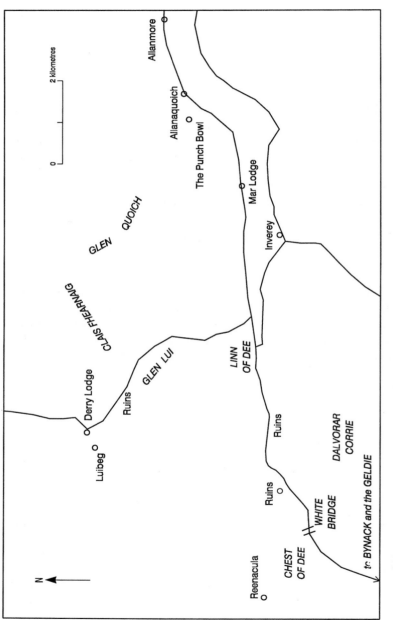

Map 14. The Cairngorm glens, with ruined townships from the Linn of Quoich to Glen Dee and Glen Lui.

# CHAPTER 14
# THE ROAD TO REENACULA

They called it Reenacula. In Gaelic it was Ruighe na Culath, the shiel of the back place, and nothing could have been more appropriate, for it was built at the back of beyond. It took its name from Coire na Culath, which lies under Sgor Mor on the approaches to the Lairig Ghru. Today, it is little more than a rickle of stones on the edge of a burn tumbling into the River Dee.

I once set out to find Reenacula, intrigued by a poem which began:

A Company as you shall hear
Of Sportsmen good, late in the year
Resolved to march, be't fair or foul, a'
From Buchan to Reenacula

It told about a party of Buchan hunters who went to Ruighe na Culath in 1816 to hunt for grouse and deer. Their cook, James Christie, wrote an epic poem about the expedition entitled 'Journal of a Hunting party from Auchry to Reenacula'. Their shiel, or bothy, stood near a narrow, heather-choked path over which they had to manoeuvre a cart carrying their luggage.

The road turn'd so rocky
on a strait hillside,
Our cart with the baggage
thought best to divide

The old shiel was thought locally to have been a small hunting lodge used by the Earls of Mar. It was on a route taken by drovers travelling through the Lairig Ghru and Glen Dee from Speyside. Shielings often doubled up as droving stances and resting places on the drove routes from the North. One shieling at Dalnaspidal, for instance, was turned into a public house for drovers when the summer grazing season was over. The Buchan deer hunters expedition to Reenacula came at a time when the shieling tradition was on the wane. They were the last of the free-ranging sportsmen. Behind them came profit-conscious lairds eager to let out their deer forests for hunting, a trend that was to accelerate the end of transhumance.

*Derry Lodge.*

The use of abandoned shiels by deer hunters became a thing of the past with the building of shooting lodges and keeper's houses. The Reenacula hunters sent their game to New Mar Lodge, originally Corriemulzie Cottage, to be carried on to Braemar. Bynack, Geldie and Derry were all built in the mid-19th century. Now Bynack and Geldie are in ruins, and Derry Lodge, boarded-up, its interior ravaged by careless hillwalkers, is on the edge of disintegration.

On the road to the Lairig Ghru, from the White Bridge to the Geldie, up the Lui Water to Derry Lodge, and down the long emptiness of Glen Ey, the Cairngorm glens have become a graveyard for old shielings, tumble-down lodges and deserted clachans. In a survey of the Mar Lodge estate, the Royal Commission on the Ancient and Historical Monuments of Scotland located the remains of twenty-two townships and about 300 shieling huts. These ruins, some barely visible in the heather, are forlorn monuments to a way of life that died out at the turn of the century.

One archaeological survey by the RCM noted two shieling clusters at the Chest of Dee, one of at least twenty-one huts, another of five heather-covered huts scattered across a series of broken terraces to the north of the waterfalls at the Chest of Dee. There was yet another shiel east of the White Bridge.

When I was exploring the townships and shielings of Glen Dee I went back to Coire na Culath, where there had been a number of shiels. Low cloud hung over 'Ben 'brotney' (Beinn Bhrotain), which Jamie Christie said was 'twa mile high' and full of 'pykie rock', and I stood there thinking of how they had lived on bread and brose, were saturated with 'wicked rain', wet all their 'sarks an' a' our duds', and fortified themselves with endless drams of whisky. Now the shooting parties drink their whisky at the laird's table.

Six miles south as the crow flies whisky glasses were raised for another reason when Queen Victoria reached the county boundary on her way home from her expedition to Blair Atholl in 1861. The Duke of Atholl, taking his leave of the Queen and Prince Albert, gave them 'some whisky to drink out of an old silver flask'.

Coming through Atholl, the Queen passed Glen Loch, where there was an area known as the Seven Shielings. One of the bothies, Ruidh na Cuile, the windy shieling, featured in a dispute with the Marquis of Athole, who believed that its use as summer grazing for cattle interfered with deer moving between his forests at Fealer and Beinn a' Ghlo. The remains of nearly thirty shiels, circular and rectangular, can still be seen there.

There was rich pastureland in Glen Loch and at the end of the 18th century some sixty families lived there during the summer months. Sheep came into their own the following century, as many as 3,500 of them grazing in the glen. Now the remains of the shiels are the only reminders of those far-off days.

When Victoria left the Duke of Atholl at the Aberdeenshire boundary she went on to the site of another well-known shiel — Bynack.'As we approached the "shiel", she wrote, 'the pipers struck up and played'. The Lodge was sometimes known as Bynack Shiel, but the name actually belonged to a shieling beside it which was originally known as Crocluch Lodge (Cro Chlach, the sheepfold of stones). At anyrate, the *real* shiels strung out along the Bynack Burn were scarcely fit for a Queen. Here, where the Geldie Burn comes bouncing in from the west, there was a heavy concentration of shieling huts; the RCAHMS calculated about forty in the area. Six groups of shieling huts lay on the east bank of the Bynack Burn from near Bynack Lodge to where it met the Geldie.

Ten years ago I met a woman who would have known them all — Nell Bynack, whose real name was Helen Macdonald. She got her by-name, like the rest of her family, because she had spent her childhood at Bynack, where her father was gamekeeper. I remember her telling me with a chuckle, 'I'm hill run'. She had been to the top of Ben Macdhui twenty-two times as an unofficial guide to hotel guests and she knew the hills like the back of her hand. One of her friends was that doyen of hillmen, Seton Gordon, the naturalist, who often stayed with her when she moved to Luibeg. The last time I heard of her she was into her nineties and living in a home in Braemar, a legendary figure who was as well-known as the famous Maggie Gruer in Inverey.

Deserted townships can be seen on both sides of the river from the Linn of Dee to the White Bridge; more from the Linn down to Allanaquoich. The RCAHMS survey recorded a total of fourteen from the White Bridge to Allanaquoich. Each has its own story. About a mile west of the Linn the Delvorar Burn runs into the Deel. In the Muckle Spate of '29 it joined the swollen Dee as it raged across the valley, sweeping round the farmhouse at Delvorar so quickly that the farmer, his wife and seven children barely had time to escape. They waded away from their home and tramped through the storm to Inverey.

Delvorar was the biggest farm in the glen. John Grant Michie said it 'carried a great stock of cattle and sheep' and that 'in the remotest parts of the Mar forest the people had their summer pasturages and shielings, full of healthy human activity'. The farm had two units, Dail a' Mhorair, the little haugh of the nobleman, and Dail a' Mhorair Mhor, the big haugh of the nobleman. Viscount Dundee camped there with his troops fourteen days before the Battle of Killiecrankie. In the late 18th century the 'double' Dalvorar had two co-tenants, but early the following century it was converted to a sheep farm. Creag Phadruig, on the north side of the Dee, takes its name from the rock face behind it, Patrick's Craig, while farther west is Tomnamoine, 'the hillock of the peat moss'. Now it is a ruin like all its neighbours.

Still farther on is Tonnagaoithe, the farthest up croft ever to be cultivated in the Dee valley. Place-name experts are divided on the meaning of the name. Adam Watson and Betty Allan said it came from Tonn na Gaoithe, 'bottom of the wind', which they took to mean bottom-land. They pointed out, however, that it was translated to them as 'winny airse', Scots for windy arse.

Dubrach, on the south bank of the river, was the birthplace of Peter Grant, the oldest surviving rebel of the '45 Jacobite Rising, who was granted a life pension by King George IV when he was 108. He lived to be 110, which seemed to throw doubt on the suggestion by the Earl of Fife's factor that the reason for the depopulation of Glen Dee was that it was never free of disease. Whatever the relevance of the factor's comments, the fact is that in 1829 only three families remained in the stretch of the Dee from the Linn to the Geldie.

Glen Lui fared no better. It is a glen of sad memories, its 'lost lands' staked out in rubble heaps along the road to Derry Lodge. 'The old people of Mar are passing from the mortal scene', wrote Seton Gordon in 1948. 'Donald Fraser of the Derry, Charles Robertson who tamed the mice in Corrour bothy, John Macintosh the piper and Sandy MacDonald of Luibeg — these men no longer climb to the high tops nor tell of the romance of ancient times.'

Gordon also wrote about these legendary figures in a much earlier book, *The Cairngorm Hills of Scotland,* published in 1925. In it, he told of how of how he had played golf with Donald Fraser in a clearing at Derry Lodge. Donald was the stalker at Derry; 'a cunning golfer', said Gordon, who had never played on any links away from his glen. Charles Robertson — 'a great character' — was deer-watcher at Corrour Bothy for the Duke of Fife. He was succeeded by John Macintosh, known as the Piper, who often played the pipes with Gordon in the bothy 'by the glow of the friendly fire of peat and bog fir'.

'That old shieling at the foot of the Devil's Point has many pleasant memories for me', wrote Gordon, but in the Cairngorm glens there were other shiels, or the ruins of them, that evoked less pleasant thoughts. He saw Glen Lui 'almost as deserted as the high Cairngorms'. All down the glen were the remains of buildings that told of a time when people had lived out their lives by the Lui Water.

Lord Grange, the Hanoverian brother of the Earl of Mar, took over the lands when they were forfeited after the '45 Rising and set about selling them to the highest bidder. In 1726 he wrote to James Farquharson of Balmoral telling him to 'eject those people after their harvest is over'. He advised Farquharson to take 'discreet men' with him who would help in the clearance...'the more you have along with you there will be the less opposition'.

Two reasons were given for the ejections. One was that it would enable 'the improvement and sale of the Timber'. The other was 'that people may see they are not to be suffered in their illegal insolence'. Lord Grange criticised James McKenzie of Dalmore for his unwillingness to help in the ejections.'Surely none of thee can be so stupid to immagine they may continue there as our Tennants in spite of our Teeth'.

The glen was re-populated about 1732, but was again cleared in 1776. Charles Cordiner, author of *Antiquaries and Scenery of the North of Scotland,* visited Glen Lui in 1776. In his book, he told of seeing 'the ruins of several stone buildings'. It showed, he said, that the glen had once been inhabited, but now, as with other pastures in the forest, had been 'left to fatten the deer'. John Grant Michie put it another way quoting a verse which spoke of great tracts of wilderness where 'the beast was ever more and more, but man was less and less'.

There are no Glen Lui settlements marked on Farquharson's map of the Forest of Mar in 1703 and Seton Gordon said that in Arrowsmith's map of 1807 there were 'at least four houses marked in Glen Lui'. Between these dates lay the clearances of 1726 and 1776.The names noted by Gordon were Knockinted and Dalgwnich on the west side of the river and Alt Vattigally and Achavadie on the east.The proper names for them were Cnoc na Teidh, Dail Gainimh, Allt a' Mhadaidh-allaidh and Ach a' Mhadaidh.

The last time I was there on a hot summer day a herd of deer had come down from the high tops, cooling themselves in the river. I could see them raising their heads, watching me suspiciously, but they stood their ground. Perhaps they knew that this was their territory.They had replaced the people.

Nowadays, hill-walkers tramping up to Derry Lodge pay scant attention to the clutter of stones just off the track.When you cross the Black Bridge and turn up towards Derry the remains of old settlements can be seen almost immediately. Away to the left near the river is a corn kiln still in good condition, while beyond the wood on the north side of the track are the ruins of a sizeable settlement. After that 'lost' townships and shielings can be traced all the way to Luibeg and up Glen Derry.

They are ugly scars on the landscape, yet once they had magical Gaelic names that told you about the places and the people... Ruighe an t-Sidhein, the cattle run of the fairy hillock (it stood beside hillocks called Na Da Shidhean), Dail Gainimh, the haugh of sand, Allt a' Mhadaidh-allaidh, the burn of the wolf, Dail Rosaigh, the haugh at the wooded place. Dail Rosaigh was a shiel before it

*Ruins near Allanaquoich. Allanmore, now deserted, can be seen in the distance.*

became a farm in the early 1740s. There were other shielings on the west side of the Lui Water following the 1726 clearance.

The Allt a' Mhadaidh, running into the Lui Water, skirts one of the ruined townships in the glen. Here, a path climbs the hill by Clais Fhearnaig, 'the little glen', and drops down to the Quoich. There are indications of shielings where the Clais Fhearnaig burn meets the Quoich and also farther up the glen. Deeper into the hills is the Beachan, where there were 'the sheallings of Milntown of Invercauld in Glenquoich of Caich' and on 'the Water of Beachan, called Usquikaich'.

To the south, where the Quoich meets the Dee, the valley opens up and the river comes winding majestically through the Dalmore haughlands. Dalmore — *Dail Mhor,* the big field — was the ancient name of Mar Lodge. There have been three Mar Lodges. The first, Old Mar Lodge, built in the 1730s by Lord Braco, stood just to the rear of the present building and the second, New Mar Lodge, was on the south side of the Dee. It was burned down in 1895 and the present Lodge was built.

There were a number of townships on the haugh around Mar Lodge in the late 17th century, but between 1763 and 1770 they

*Allanmore, shuttered and deserted.*

were cleared by the Earl of Fife so that he could enjoy an uninterrupted view around the lodge. The ruins of Tom nan Sealgair, lying between Claybokie and Mar Lodge, are thought to have been cleared during work on the road to the Linn of Quoich. Near Mar Lodge was Baile nan Taobhanach, a name that meant the farm-town of the rafters, while Ceann na Dalach was a house and chapel also near the Lodge.

East of Mar Lodge was Allanaquoich, which in 1696 had five tenants and twelve sub-tenants. Both it and a sister settlement, Ceann na Coille, were cleared in the late 18th and early 19th centuries and let to a single tenant. The clearance of Cragan and Little or Wester Allanaquoich by 1790 followed moves by the Earl of Fife to rid himself of tenants who would not adapt to modern farming methods. Tenants to be removed were listed in a memorandum of 1782.

About a mile and a half east of the Linn of Quoich is the farm of Allanmore, its farmhouse boarded up and deserted, its twin chimneys adding a touch of Victorian charm to its creeping dereliction. A red-roofed bothy nearby looked as if it had been abandoned in a hurry, as if its occupants had suddenly walked out on it. The wooden frame of a bed lay in one corner, a kist on top of it, a suitcase in another corner, the frame of a man's bike on the floor.

*The abandoned bothy at Allanmore.*

Intriguingly, the frame of a woman's bicycle lay outside. Whoever owned them had long since gone — Allanmore had become another 'lost' township. It looked as if history was repeating itself, for there had been another fermtoun there before it. All around the farmhouse were the foundations of earlier buildings.

It was at the Quoich that my journey came to an end. Different theories have been put forward about the meaning of the word Quoich or Caich. One is that it comes from *cuach,* a quaich or bowl, in this case the Earl of Mar's Punchbowl, where Jacobite toasts were drunk in 'ankers of potent Aquavitae' poured into the bowl. But some place-name experts have discounted this explanation.

A number of possibilities are given in *The Place Names of Upper Deeside,* among them *Cothaich* (strive) and *Cath* (battle or struggle). To strive, to struggle...they were words that might have been applied to what I saw in my wanderings in the North-east. I had tramped through the Cabrach, the 'backside of the world'; had seen the shielings of Strathaven and the wonders of Ruighe Speanan; and had found my way into remote and little-known corners of Deeside and Donside. The ruins of countless townships had testified to an endless struggle against poverty and disease, against the clearances and the 'ill years'; against homes that were 'shocking to humanity' and against lairds who thought that the peasant's dream of a better life was nothing more than 'Illegal Insolence'.

They were the people I was thinking of when I stood at the Earl of Mar's Punchbowl. My toast was for them, for the crofters and cottars, the grassers and herd boys, the weavers and souters...for all those forgotten generations who had once lived out their lives in the Land of the Lost.

# INDEX

# INDEX